From Blueprint to Reality: San Diego's Education Reforms

• • •

Julian R. Betts
Andrew C. Zau
Kevin King

2005

Library of Congress Cataloging-in-Publication Data

Betts, Julian R.

From blueprint to reality : San Diego's education reforms / Julian R. Betts, Andrew Zau, Kevin King.

p. cm.

Includes bibliographical references.

ISBN-13: 978-1-58213-105-4

ISBN: 1-58213-105-8

1. Educational equalization—California—San Diego. 2. Blueprint for Student Success (Program)—Evaluation. 3. Academic achievement—California—San Diego. 4. San Diego City Schools— Evaluation. 5. School improvement programs—California—San Diego. 6. Educational indicators—California—San Diego. I. Zau, Andrew. II. King, Kevin, 1975- III. Title.

LC213.23.S26B47 2005

371.2009794'985—dc22

2005025039

San Francisco, CA

PPIC does not take or support positions on any ballot measure or on any local, state, or federal legislation, nor does it endorse, support, or oppose any political parties or candidates for public office.

Research publications reflect the views of the authors and do not necessarily reflect the views of the staff, officers, or Board of Directors of the Public Policy Institute of California.

Foreword

In 2000, the Public Policy of Institute of California entered into an agreement with the San Diego Unified School District to provide the research and financial support to collect, format, and analyze student, teacher, and classroom data needed to create an accurate portrait of what affects student achievement in San Diego. This report, authored by Julian R. Betts, Andrew C. Zau, and Kevin King is the second in a series stemming from that agreement. Most important, it is a report that throws new light on the school district's program of reform known as the Blueprint for Student Success. The report was made possible by grants from The William and Flora Hewlett Foundation and The Atlantic Philanthropies.

The Blueprint was both visionary and controversial. It was visionary because it focused on improving reading skills while encompassing virtually all of the district's students and teachers, and controversial because its implementation drew both severe criticism from professional staff, parents, and community organizations but also support from other parent groups and the business community. Education specialists and nonprofit organizations throughout the country have watched the San Diego Blueprint with great interest—some even providing substantial financial support to implement comprehensive teacher training programs. As a result, serious assessments of student performance during the years of the reform effort will be reviewed with great interest. Given the quality of their data, this report by Betts, Zau, and King is worthy of special attention.

The authors conclude that the effort to improve reading skills was successful and that the evidence for the program's overall success is so definitive that San Diego's efforts are well worth a look by other school districts in California and the nation. A significant percentage of elementary and middle school students who took part in reform-driven activities—such as double- and triple-length English classes, extended school days, and summer school reading programs—showed marked improvement on standardized reading tests. High school students did not experience the same test improvements and various reasons for this result are discussed. Nevertheless, to show such consistent gains in reading performance across the elementary and middle school grades is worth note and offers some lessons for other school systems in the country.

Many of the programs that were part of the Blueprint have subsequently been reduced in scale or shut down entirely. Yet the effects of the Blueprint may be measurable for years to come—only future research will reveal whether its effects are long-lasting. But the authors conclude that the individual programs are less important than the Blueprint's broader principles: Use reading assessments to identify students who lag behind, strongly encourage families of these students to enroll them in additional literacy classes during the school year or in the summer, and do everything possible to ensure that teachers are fully trained in techniques to improve literacy. The unusually detailed student-level analysis underlying this report provides strong evidence that reforms such as these can produce meaningful reductions in the achievement gap. This evidence deserves serious national attention.

David W. Lyon
President and CEO
Public Policy Institute of California

Summary

If the trend toward student testing in the United States has taught us one thing, it is that achievement gaps by race, parental education, and parental income are large and persistent.

Prodded by these stubborn achievement gaps, virtually all state governments have recently implemented school accountability systems. For instance, in 1999, California implemented the Public School Accountability Act, which mandates state content standards (that is, a specific body of knowledge and skills that students are expected to master at each grade), student testing, and a school-level accountability system. This trend has gained further momentum with the passage in 2001 of the federal No Child Left Behind (NCLB) Act. A key aspect of both federal and state systems is an emphasis on reducing the large gaps in achievement that exist when students' scores are grouped by race or parental income.

The creation of school accountability systems represents a helpful step forward, but it has left school districts scrambling to find ways to boost overall achievement and to narrow the achievement gaps in their schools. There is growing evidence that simply "spending more" across all schools has done little to boost test scores or to narrow achievement gaps. Policymakers are increasingly coming to the conclusion that districts need to implement far more aggressive reforms to improve the status quo.

A number of large urban districts have started to implement reforms that focus on students who lag behind. One of the most important among these efforts is taking place in the San Diego Unified School District (SDUSD), which formally launched its Blueprint for Student Success in summer 2000. The plan calls for massive redeployment of educational resources to help students who are identified by test scores as underachieving, with an initial focus on reading.

The reform is remarkable both for its scope and the controversy it has generated. Marshall Smith, former U.S. Under Secretary of Education and currently Program Director for Education of the Hewlett Foundation, told the *San Diego Union Tribune*: "This really is the most important urban school reform effort in the country. . . . If the reforms work here they will have a national effect because ideas travel." Another reason for the plan receiving national attention is the sheer size of the district, which is the second largest in California and the eighth largest in the nation. The district has received tens of millions of dollars from a number of foundations to help implement the reforms, and former U.S. Secretary of Education Rod Paige has publicly supported the district's efforts.

Locally, the reforms have generated intense controversy. Surveys by the American Institutes for Research found that the majority of teachers opposed many aspects of the reforms, and local parent groups are divided on whether the reforms merely relegate the students most in need to tracked classes, or instead provide useful and much needed help to these same students.

This report seeks to provide the first student-level analysis of the effect of the Blueprint reforms. It studies the school years 1999–2000 through 2001–2002. We chose these years because the district formally introduced the Blueprint in summer 2000, with very partial implementation of some components of the reform in the fall 1999 to spring 2000 (1999–2000) school year.

The overall objectives of this research project are fourfold. First, we examine how many students have participated in each intervention in the first two years. Second, we study the effect of the Blueprint reforms on average reading achievement and on the gap in reading achievement between racial/ethnic groups and between groups defined by socioeconomic and language status. Third, we explore the mechanisms through which the Blueprint has worked most and least effectively. Our fourth goal is to provide policy advice. With a new superintendent, Dr. Carl A. Cohn, arriving in the district in October 2005, the Blueprint is very much at a crossroads. Clearly, a careful retrospective analysis of what did and did not work is essential. Given the national attention that the Blueprint has received, we believe that our findings can also assist other districts statewide and nationwide as they design education reform plans of their own.

Summary of Blueprint Reforms

In 1998, Superintendent Alan Bersin enlisted the help of Chancellor of Instruction Tony Alvarado to develop and implement the Blueprint. Chancellor Alvarado adapted some of the reading reforms that he had previously introduced as superintendent of Community School District #2 in New York. The Blueprint that emerged in San Diego emphasizes the concept of "Balanced Literacy," which calls for teachers to promote reading "by, with and to children," with teachers becoming more actively involved as they introduce more difficult text to their students.

The Blueprint boils down to three main strategies that place the priority on a student's literacy abilities. The first strategy is *prevention*. This strategy applies to all students and teachers and focuses on enhanced teaching of students, extensive training of teachers, and innovative classroom materials. The second strategy is *intervention.* Teachers identify students performing below grade level who then receive extra instruction through programs including extra-length English classes, an extended day, or summer school and more focused teacher training in literacy, depending on the student's needs. The final strategy is *retention*, that is, the practice of having a student repeat a grade with accelerated support. A common thread across these strategies is extra time on task for students, with a focus on the basics of reading and writing rather than a pure focus on literature. All of this is backed by professional development for teachers that was designed to help teachers choose appropriate teaching strategies for students at various levels of literacy. However, the Blueprint is in general not prescriptive in the sense of requiring that teachers teach from specific texts at specific times.

Initially, the interventions have focused primarily on reading. More recently, similar elements related to mathematics have been developed as well but on a far smaller scale. Thus, this report focuses on the effect of the Blueprint on reading achievement. We now describe all of the Blueprint elements. As we note below, some of these elements have recently been discontinued.

Prevention Strategies

The prevention strategies for all students that were in place in the first year, 2000–2001, included:

- Use of a new literacy framework in all grades,
- "Enhanced classes" in the sense of additional teaching materials for all kindergarten and grade 1 teachers,
- One or two peer coaches for all schools, to help teachers learn proven teaching methods, and
- "Genre studies" consisting of a two-period English class for all students in the entering grade of middle or junior high school who are near to, at, or above grade level, with related professional development for their teachers.

Students below the category of near grade level in certain grades received more intensive versions of genre studies, as we will describe below.

In addition, focus schools (the elementary schools with the weakest scores in the state test, ranking in the bottom tenth statewide) received an extended school year, a second peer coach, and other funds and staff. The elementary schools that ranked in the second-lowest decile of the state ranks, known as "API 2" schools, received a second peer coach and additional funds but not an extended school year.[1]

Intervention and Grade Retention Strategies

The second category of Blueprint reforms is a detailed set of interventions. Unlike the preventive measures, the interventions are targeted at specific groups of students. Decisions about who receives these interventions are based upon student test results. Students "below grade level" or "significantly below grade level" were eligible for slightly different interventions. The key intervention strategies were

---

[1]API is the acronym for the Academic Performance Index, a statistic measuring overall student achievement in a school. The California Department of Education calculates the API for each school annually. It also ranks schools into ten API deciles. Hence API 2 schools rank in the second-lowest decile of achievement statewide.

- Literacy block. Literacy block is a double-length English language class offered in grades 6 through 10. This variant of genre studies is given to students who lag below or significantly below grade level.
- Literacy core. For students significantly below grade level in grade 9, the literacy-block class is extended to three periods. In 2001–2002, grade 6 and 7 students also began to participate in literacy core.
- Extended Day Reading Program (EDRP). In all schools with grades 1–9, students below and significantly below grade level receive three 90-minute periods each week of supervised reading before or after school.
- Summer school. In addition to the standard summer school for students who have failed courses, Blueprint summer school is aimed at students in most grades from K through 9 who lag below and significantly below grade level. Students are asked to attend for six weeks, for four hours per day.[2] Some schools in the district, mostly elementary schools, are year-round schools at which the schedules did not permit the implementation of Blueprint summer school. At these schools, students in affected grades who lagged behind in reading participated in special intersession studies.
- Grade retention. In extreme cases, students were asked to repeat a grade and were given additional tutoring in the year that they repeated the grade. Grade retention was limited to entry-level grades of elementary and middle school/junior high school: grades 1, 6 in middle school, and 7 in junior high school.

Data and Methods

This research builds on a database constructed for the first PPIC report on student achievement in San Diego, titled *Determinants of Student Achievement: New Evidence from San Diego,* by Betts, Zau, and Rice (2003). This earlier report compiled longitudinal data on student

---

[2]In addition, all secondary school students with D/F grades attend a more traditional type of summer school consisting of six weeks of courses in core subjects.

records and in addition linked these records with information on the qualifications of the teachers in each classroom. This database was augmented by adding variables indicating whether students had participated in each of the specific Blueprint interventions and also by measuring the school-level preventive measures described above. The data were updated to the 2001–2002 school year to provide a full picture of the effect of the Blueprint in its first two years.

Because we have multiple years of data for most students, we can allow for the fact that the learning trajectories of any two children are likely to differ. In effect, each student becomes his own "comparison group" because we test whether the student learns more in the years that he participates in a given intervention, relative to years in which he does not. By including a year of data before the main Blueprint elements were introduced in summer 2000, we can compare growth in achievement before and after the interventions were initiated.

Similarly, we control for unobserved but fixed characteristics of the student's home zip code and his school. The latter is particularly important for assessing the effect of a school being designated a focus or API 2 school. We want to know whether something positive happens to student achievement in those years that a focus or API 2 school receives additional support from the district, above and beyond the pre-existing trend in student achievement at these schools.

Patterns of Student Participation in Blueprint Interventions

The district has targeted the various interventions in a quite focused way. In both 2000–2001 and 2001–2002, roughly one-third of students participated in at least one intervention. We found that EDRP and literacy block both garnered the highest participation rate at around 25 percent of students in relevant grades. Blueprint grade retention, which debuted in 2001–2002, was the least common intervention, at 1.3 percent of students in the relevant grades.

Participants in the four student-based interventions that we studied are much more likely to be nonwhite or English Learners (ELs) or to have parents with relatively low education. For instance, one out of two

English Learners participated in literacy block on average, compared to fewer than one out of five fluent English-speaking students. As shown in Figure S.1, participation rates in EDRP and Blueprint summer school were far higher among students whose parents had relatively little education. Among races and ethnicities, we found that whites uniformly were least likely to participate in interventions and that Hispanics were the most likely. For instance, in the relevant grades, 8.9 percent of whites participated in literacy block compared to 38.7 percent of Hispanics.

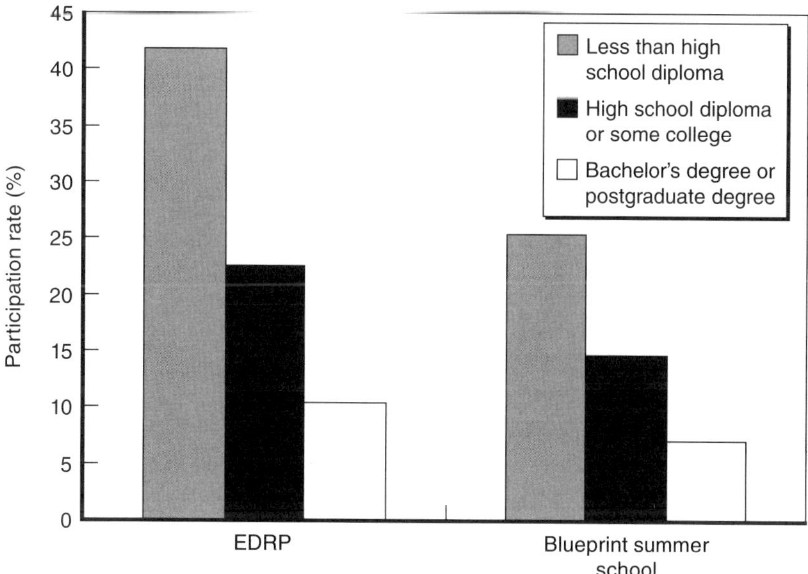

NOTE: Rates are calculated based on all students in relevant grades in either 2000–2001 or 2001–2002 and thus are an enrollment-weighted average of participation in the two years.

Figure S.1—Student Participation Rates in Extended Day Reading Program and Blueprint Summer School by the Level of Education of the Student's More Highly Educated Parent

Were the "Right" Students Assigned to Blueprint Interventions?

The district has used reading test scores to assign students to interventions very much as announced. However, test scores alone seldom determine placement of students. Test scores were most important in determining assignments to literacy block and core, where students whose scores suggested they were eligible were typically 12 to 77 times as likely to participate as students whose reading scores officially exempted them. Test scores were typically the least influential in determining assignment to Blueprint grade retention, in that many students whose scores made them eligible for retention were nonetheless promoted to the next grade.

Our finding that there is some flexibility in the assignment process matches official district policy in the sense that teachers and parents have input into assignment decisions, and this is particularly so for grade retention. It is also clear that EDRP and Blueprint summer school have lower participation rates among eligible students than do literacy block and core. Also, with the exception of grade retention, occasionally students who are slightly above the official test score cutoff participate in an intervention. Teacher recommendations as well as the need to fill out classes explain the phenomenon.

Overall, we found clear evidence that the district uses achievement scores as announced, but there is considerable flexibility in practice.

The Overall Effect of the Blueprint on Student Achievement

The main result of our statistical analysis is that, overall, the Blueprint had a statistically significant effect on student achievement in reading, but these effects varied dramatically by grade level. The Blueprint had a large positive effect on students' reading gains in elementary schools, a smaller but still positive effect in middle schools, and, overall, a moderate *negative* effect on reading gains among high school students.

We arrived at these conclusions by combining two pieces of evidence: first, our statistical regressions that modeled an individual student's achievement gains as a function of Blueprint variables and other variables, and, second, data identifying which students participated in each Blueprint element. Specifically, we followed over a two-year period all students who entered grades 3, 6, and 9 in fall 2000. We measured their participation in each aspect of the Blueprint over the period from summer 2000 to spring 2002. We identified where these students finished in the district's own distribution of test scores in spring 2002 and then asked the counterfactual question: "Where would these students have ranked if the Blueprint had not existed?" To answer this question, we divided students in these three grade cohorts into ten equally sized groups, or deciles, based on their spring 2002 reading test scores.

Figure S.2 shows the results for elementary school students. The dark bars show where these Blueprint participants would have ranked without the Blueprint. In a world without the Blueprint, the vast majority of these students would have been in the bottom five deciles, which is not surprising, given that the district's assessment tools had

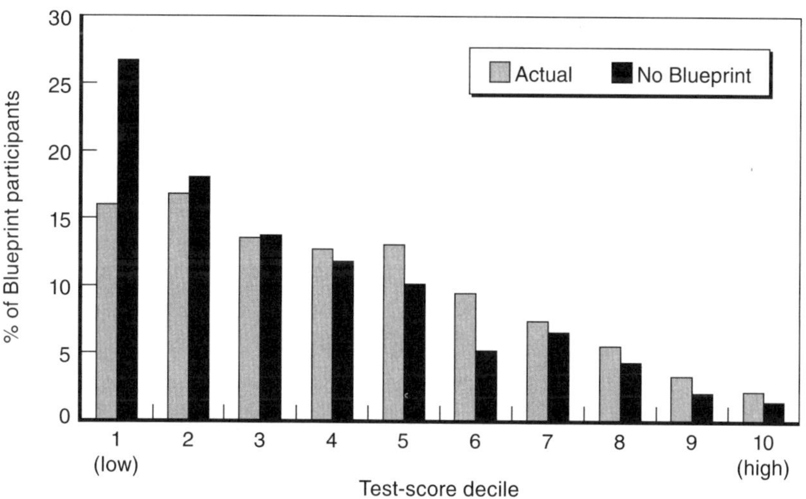

Figure S.2—Distribution of Fall 2000 Grade 3 Blueprint Participants by Spring 2002 Test-Score Decile: Actual and Simulated Distribution Without Blueprint

previously identified these students as lagging behind. The lighter colored bars show where these students actually ended up in the test score distribution after having participated in the Blueprint. **The differences are quite striking: Our results suggest that the Blueprint shifted well over 10 percent of these students out of the bottom two deciles of reading achievement and into higher deciles.**

Results for middle schools are similar but more modest, with just over 4 percent of participants being shifted out of the bottom two deciles of test-score performance. High school results display a perverse result: The Blueprint is predicted to have shifted just under 5 percent of participants *into* the two lowest deciles of test-score performance.

With the major exception of high school, then, we conclude that the Blueprint reforms meaningfully increased gains in reading.

The Effect of the Blueprint on Achievement Gaps

We followed the same three cohorts over two years and estimated how the Blueprint affected the initial test score gaps related to language, race/ethnicity, and parental education.

We find evidence that in elementary and to a lesser extent middle schools, the Blueprint narrowed achievement gaps defined along racial/ethnic, language, and socioeconomic lines. However, the opposite is true in high schools.

In elementary schools, all three ways in which we grouped students suggest that the Blueprint led to quite substantial reductions in the achievement gap. Most impressive in this regard were the EL/non-EL gap, the Hispanic/white gap, and the gap between students whose more highly educated parent was a high school dropout and students who had at least one parent whose education continued beyond the bachelor's degree level. Each of these gaps is estimated to have shrunk by about 15 percent over two years because of the Blueprint.

Middle school results similarly suggest that the Blueprint reduced the various achievement gaps, but by less than 5 percent. High school results are uniformly negative in that they suggest the Blueprint widened achievement gaps. The most dramatic instance was the high school EL/non-EL gap, which is predicted to have widened by roughly 10 percent. Figure S.3 shows the changes in the initial gap in reading

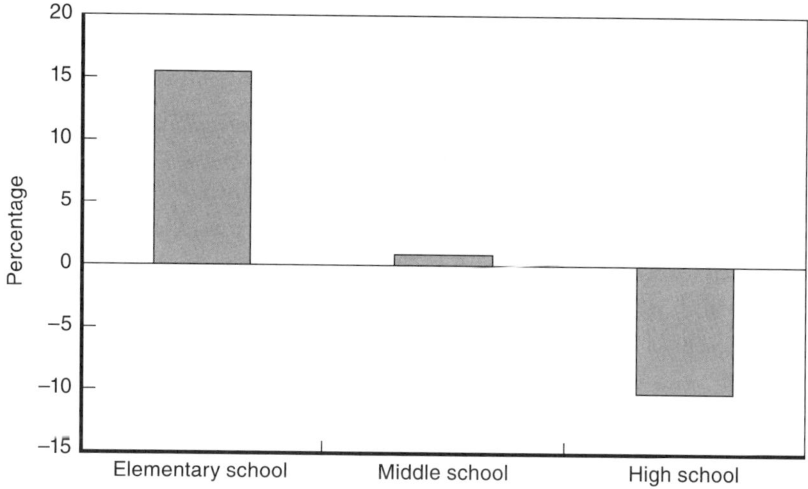

NOTE: The figure shows the predicted two-year reduction in test-score gap between spring 2000 and spring 2002 for students in grades 3, 6, and 9 in fall 2000. A positive/negative bar indicates that the initial gap is predicted to have narrowed/widened as a result of the Blueprint.

Figure S.3—Two-Year Reduction in EL/Non-EL Test-Score Gaps Attributable to the Blueprint

achievement between EL and non-EL students, again showing that high schools bucked the pattern of reduced achievement gaps observed in lower grades.

Which Blueprint Elements Have Influenced Student Gains in Reading?

It is important to bear in mind that with only two years of data for most Blueprint elements (genre studies and literacy block were phased in on a very limited basis in 1999–2000, and peer coaches were quite widely introduced in this year as well), it is certainly possible that we lack enough data to detect effects of the reforms. An analysis suggests that the one Blueprint variable for which we are very unlikely to be able to detect meaningful effects is Blueprint grade retention, which began on a very small scale in the last year of our sample.

With this warning in mind, it is quite remarkable how many of the Blueprint variables proved to be highly statistically significant. (By "statistically significant" we mean that it is very unlikely that the true effect of these Blueprint elements was zero.)

The effect of peer coaches is typically not statistically significant, and in a few cases may have been weakly negative. Peer coach *experience* did not seem to change the effect of the peer-coach-to-enrollment ratio.

In contrast, the funneling of targeted resources toward focus and API 2 elementary schools beginning in fall 2000 appears to have had a positive and highly significant effect. Similarly, EDRP and Blueprint summer school both are positive and statistically significant in each of the gradespans in which they are offered.

The special double- and triple-length English classes, when compared to regular single-period English classes, seem to have had quite different effects at the middle and high school levels. We could detect no effect of genre studies on students at the middle school level. (Genre studies, sometimes referred to as Enhanced Literacy, are the *preventive* double-length English classes that are targeted at students who were near, at, or above grade level.) In contrast, both the literacy block and core *interventions* that are aimed at students below and significantly below grade level were very strongly associated with gains in reading achievement. At the high school level, in contrast, literacy block for non-EL students, and block/core as a whole for EL students, were strongly associated with smaller reading gains, and literacy core was not statistically different from single-period English classes in its effect on non-EL students.

For the most part, we found that the estimated effect of these Blueprint variables did not depend on the teacher's experience.

How Big Is the Effect of Specific Blueprint Elements on Gains in Reading?

We gauged the size of the effect of the Blueprint on students' reading achievement in several ways. First we predicted the effect of participating in a given Blueprint element by dividing the predicted gain in test scores by the average annual gain in test scores we observe for all students in the same gradespan.

Figures S.4 through S.6 show results for elementary, middle, and high schools, respectively. Each figure shows for each Blueprint element that was statistically significant the predicted effects on average gains in reading achievement. The height of each bar corresponds to the percentage change in annual gains in achievement related to each Blueprint element. These figures suggest that, overall, the effects of the various Blueprint elements have been quite large. The reforms appear to have boosted gains in test scores substantially in elementary schools. For instance, Figure S.4 shows that participation in the reforms specific to either a focus or API 2 elementary school, or participation in Blueprint summer school, is predicted to boost a student's annual reading gains by over 10 percent each, and the effect of EDRP is just below 10 percent. The Blueprint reforms also appear to have boosted scores moderately in middle schools but depressed reading achievement in high schools.

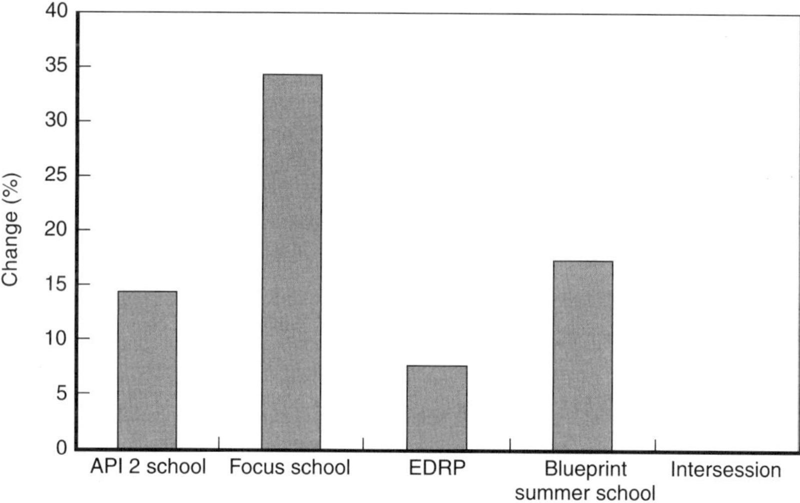

NOTES: A bar with a height of zero indicates no statistically significant effect. See Table 4.3 for a full list of insignificant Blueprint elements.

Figure S.4—Predicted Effect of Blueprint Elements on Annual Gains in Reading Achievement Among Elementary School Students

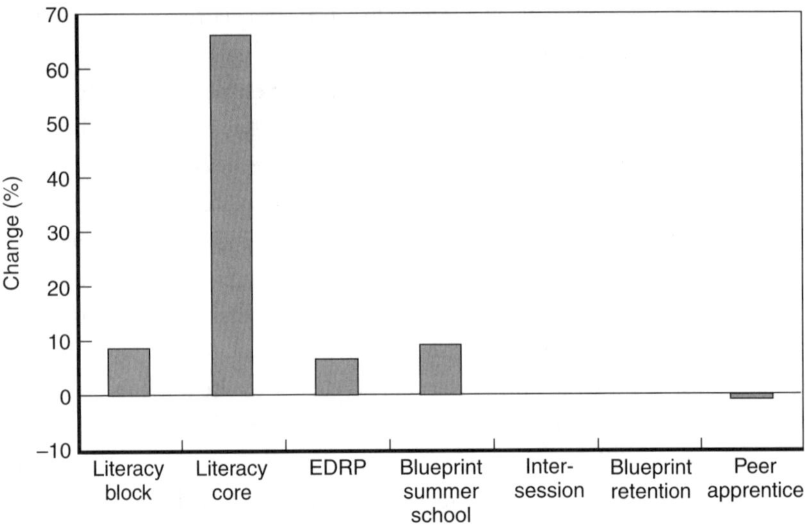

NOTES: A bar with a height of zero indicates no statistically significant effect. See Table 4.3 for a full list of insignificant Blueprint elements. For peer apprentice coaches as a percentage of enrollment, we simulated the effect of changing from zero to the mean number of peer apprentice coaches (as a percentage of enrollment). The lack of significance of Blueprint retention reported for middle schools could reflect lack of variation in our data.

Figure S.5—Predicted Effect of Blueprint Elements on Annual Gains in Reading Achievement Among Middle School Students

Some of the predicted declines at the high school level are quite large in percentage terms, but because throughout California average reading score gains are typically quite low in high school, a small absolute effect is typically quite big as a percentage of growth.

There are also some common findings across gradespans. The Extended Day Reading Program appears to have boosted student achievement in both middle and elementary schools. Blueprint summer school, the lone intervention that is offered in all three gradespans, has appeared to contribute to growth in reading achievement in all of these gradespans.[3]

[3]In the period under study in SDUSD, average annual gains in reading achievement for individual students were 25.7 points in elementary schools, 14.7 points in middle schools, and 3.3 points in high schools. So, for example, if participating in a specific Blueprint option in elementary school is predicted to boost reading scores by 5 points, we

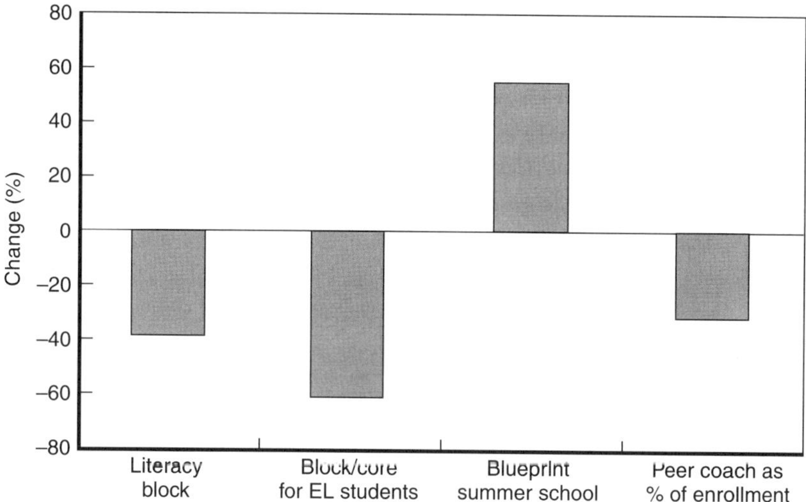

NOTES: See Table 4.3 for a full list of insignificant Blueprint elements. For peer coaches as a percentage of enrollment, we simulated the effect of changing from zero to the mean percentage of peer coaches. Because the variable "Block/core for EL students" was measured for EL students only, the predicted effect on gains in reading achievement was calculated relative to EL high school students' average annual gains—6.54 points, compared to 3.3 points for the overall population.

Figure S.6—Predicted Effect of Blueprint Elements on Annual Gains in Reading Achievement Among High School Students

Testing for Variations by Year in the Effectiveness of the Blueprint

We have found some evidence that the overall effect of the Blueprint's elements has improved over time, most strongly in elementary schools and to a lesser extent in high schools. Results in middle schools were more mixed. The evidence implies that as the district has gained experience with the various reforms, the reforms have on the whole become more effective. Most notably, as mentioned above,

---

would estimate the predicted percentage gain by dividing 5 by the average gain of 25.7, yielding a predicted gain in achievement of 19.5 percent. We note that the gains in reading scores tail off considerably in the higher grades, a pattern seen throughout California. A practical implication for our simulations is that at the high-school level, the same *absolute* effect of 5 points can produce an eye-popping change in *percentage* terms.

overall peer coaching in elementary schools had an effect that was not statistically different from zero. We find some evidence that this overall zero effect consists of a negative effect in 1999–2000 and a small positive effect in later years. Similarly, the negative effect of literacy core and block in high schools appears to have improved to a zero effect by 2001–2002. It will take several more years of data to know for sure whether these apparent trends are genuine or simply random short-term variations.

Testing for Possible Side Effects of the Blueprint on Outcomes Apart from Reading

We tested for two possible side effects of the Blueprint. The first is that the Blueprint's initial emphasis on reading could potentially have lowered student learning in the other key subject of math. We label this the "academic diversion" hypothesis. The second potential side effect is that the additional time students were asked to devote to reading could have induced "burn-out" of students in terms of increased student absences.

We found some evidence contradicting the notion that the Blueprint's reading programs have hurt math achievement. At the elementary and middle school levels, participation in various Blueprint elements designed to improve reading was often associated with 5 to 15 percent gains in the average rate of math achievement growth. These findings support the opposing hypothesis that reading ability is a "gateway" skill that can foster student learning in other subjects. In contrast, high school results were mixed. Literacy core was associated with a drop of about one half in gains in math. In a sense, this mimics the results for reading gains, suggesting the Blueprint reforms have had far more beneficial effects in lower grades than in upper grades.

Our test of the burn-out hypothesis—the idea that the Blueprint has encouraged student absences—suggested that quite the opposite was occurring at the elementary school level. Here, student exposure to Blueprint reading reforms was uniformly predicted to reduce student absences. At the middle and high school levels, results varied, suggesting the lack of a consistent effect.

Conclusion and Tentative Implications for Policy

Overall, did the reforms work? How large were the effects? And why do we see variations in effectiveness? We found evidence that in its first two years, the Blueprint led to significant gains in achievement in elementary and, to a lesser extent, middle schools. Both schoolwide preventive strategies such as the focus and API 2 elementary school programs, and interventions narrowly targeted to individual students across all schools, such as the Extended Day Reading Program and Blueprint summer school, appear to have worked well. Clearly, the biggest disappointment in these initial results is that the large and positive results in elementary and middle schools have not transferred to the high school setting. Only Blueprint summer school appears to have worked as intended at the high school level.

On the question of why we see variations in effectiveness, the very successful focus and API 2 programs at elementary schools largely explain why the Blueprint worked better at elementary schools than middle schools.

As for the overall negative results at the high school level, we have four hypotheses about why the high school experience with literacy block and core was so much more negative than it was in elementary and middle schools. In brief, less personal contact between individual teachers and students at the high school level may make it more difficult for teachers to diagnose and solve reading problems. Second, high school English teachers may have been better prepared than their counterparts in earlier grades to teach literature than to teach remedial literacy skills. Third, Chancellor Alvarado's reforms, which were adapted from his earlier experience in a K–8 district in New York, had not been deployed in a high school setting before, implying that the reforms had yet to be fine-tuned at the high school level. We could therefore reasonably expect a relatively less effective implementation in the uncharted territory of San Diego's high schools and, possibly, some improvement over time as high school teachers and administrators gain experience. In fact, we did observe evidence at the high school level that two of the Blueprint interventions initially had a negative influence on high school student reading, which improved to a zero influence by

2001–2002. Fourth, teenagers at the high school level may have felt negatively stigmatized by the pull-out English classes at a time when peers were instead enrolling in college preparatory classes.

One way to infer tentative policy conclusions is to summarize how the district has altered the Blueprint since its inception in fall 2000. Partly because of slower test score gains in the higher grades, as of 2004–2005 the district no longer offered literacy core in middle or high schools. In 2005, the district's board also acted to dismantle the peer coach program. The district in fact began in 2003–2004 to supplement peer coaches with "content-level administrators" in literacy, math, and science, who focused more on content and less on pedagogy than peer coaches. Pressure to reduce budgets in tight financial times has also had an influence, leading the district to severely curtail EDRP in fall 2003. Less dramatically, Blueprint summer school, which still exists, has faced some limits on availability.

Cutting back literacy core in high school garners more support from our results than does cutting it back in middle school. Indeed, we found positive and significant effects of literacy core in middle school, unlike high school. Although we emphasize that our results are based on only the first two years of these programs, they suggest that eliminating literacy core, especially in middle schools, may have been premature.

Similarly, our results found that EDRP benefited students meaningfully in both elementary and middle schools. This suggests that the recent curtailment of this program is unfortunate. Further, a very rough benefit-cost calculation suggests that EDRP was relatively much more cost-effective than some of the other reforms. This finding suggests that restoring EDRP, or some variant, to its original scope should perhaps be a priority when the budget outlook improves.

One element of the Blueprint reforms that had yet to show a clear effect on student learning is the peer coach program. We argue that this component of the reforms may take some time to bear fruit. It is only as peer coaches spend more time interacting with classroom teachers that we could expect this important aspect of professional development to affect the classroom tangibly. Although we found some evidence that peer coaching was beginning to yield dividends in elementary schools by

2001–2002, overall it appears that peer coaching was not initially one of the most cost-effective elements of the reform.

For readers in the rest of California and the nation, what do our results suggest? In particular given that SDUSD Superintendent Alan Bersin left San Diego on July 1, 2005, to become California's new Secretary of Education, what lessons can he, and should he, take from San Diego to inform his new role in Sacramento? Should the Blueprint be copied elsewhere in California?

First, our findings suggest that systemic reform at all levels from the district offices down to the individual classroom and student can and does work. Second, the findings tentatively suggest that elements of the Blueprint might serve as the basis for reforms elsewhere in California and the country, at least at the elementary and middle school levels. However, our initial results suggest that the state needs to look elsewhere for more successful models of literacy reform at the high school level.

Both in San Diego and elsewhere, policymakers will need to dig much deeper than these overall conclusions in deciding which elements deserve to survive in some form in San Diego and to be emulated elsewhere. The Blueprint's interwoven marriage of professional development programs for teachers and detailed interventions for students at risk is complex. We have found the most successful elements of the reforms to be the Extended Day Reading Program, summer school, elementary focus schools with their longer school year, and (at least in middle schools) extended length classes. At their heart, all of these programs share three simple principles:

1. Use reading assessments to identify students (or entire schools) lagging seriously behind in reading,
2. Strongly encourage families of these students to enroll them in additional literacy classes, whether during the school day, after school, or in summer, and
3. Do all that is possible to make sure that the teachers at the front of these students' classrooms are fully trained in literacy techniques.

In San Diego, teachers are clearly divided on whether the district succeeded in this last task. But put together, these three rules—regular assessment of students, targeting of additional literacy activities to students found to be lagging behind, and professional development of their teachers—speak to a clarity of mission and a singleness of purpose. For other districts around the state and country, which are now struggling to eradicate their own achievement gaps to satisfy both state and federal school accountability mandates, the overall direction of the Blueprint deserves serious attention.

Contents

Figures

Tables

Acknowledgments

This research project is a product of a multiyear collaboration with many departments within the San Diego Unified School District. It has been a pleasure to work with everyone at the district. We would like to thank former Superintendent Alan Bersin, now Secretary of Education for California, for the opportunity to study this very interesting and challenging topic. We are particularly grateful for the assistance provided by Karen Bachofer, who unstintingly provided her time to review our research plans and share her insights on results. We would like to thank Peter Bell, Sally Bennett, Jeff Jones, Dina Policar, Leah Baylon, and Gary Knowles from the Research and Reporting Department. We also benefited from the help of Debbie Broderick and Pia Reyes from the Extended Learning Opportunities Department.

We would like to acknowledge the generous financial support of The William and Flora Hewlett Foundation and The Atlantic Philanthropies, which have funded this Blueprint project. We would particularly like to thank Marshall Smith, Program Director for the Education Program at The William and Flora Hewlett Foundation for his enthusiasm for this project and for his valuable insights. We also warmly acknowledge the Public Policy Institute of California, which provided the financial support that led to the first PPIC report on San Diego schools in 2003, and without which the infrastructure for the current project would not have existed. In addition, at the University of California, San Diego, Dean of Social Sciences Paul Drake has kindly provided space for the overall SDUSD project since its inception in 2000. Without all of this support, this report would not have been possible.

Finally, we are indebted to our reviewers, Tracy Gordon, Henry Levin, Paul G. Lewis, Margaret Raymond, and Jon Sonstelie, as well as to our editors, Gary Bjork, Joyce Peterson, and Patricia Bedrosian for many helpful suggestions.

Any opinions or interpretations expressed in this report are those of the authors alone and do not necessarily reflect the views of the Public Policy Institute of California.

Acronyms

API	Academic Performance Index
ARI	Analytical Reading Inventory
BCLAD	Bilingual Crosscultural Language and Academic Development
CBEDS	California Basic Educational Data System
CCTC	California Commission on Teacher Credentialing
CLAD	Crosscultural Language and Academic Development
CSR	Class Size Reduction
CSU	California State University
DRA	Developmental Reading Assessment
EDRP	Extended Day Reading Program
EL	English Learner
FEP	Fluent English Proficient
LAE	Limited Assignment Emergency
LAUSD	Los Angeles Unified School District
NCLB	No Child Left Behind
SDRT	Stanford Diagnostic Reading Test
SDUSD	San Diego Unified School District
UC	University of California

1. Introduction

In 1983, a national commission released *A Nation at Risk*, a clarion cry for the need to improve public schooling in America.[1] Partly in response to this scathing report, states have moved to introduce student testing systems. These testing systems, although controversial, have performed a public service by exposing large and persistent achievement gaps related to race, parental education, and parental income. For example, Jencks and Phillips (1998) provide a well-known survey of the black-white achievement gap.

In a California context, Betts, Rueben, and Danenberg (2000) and Sonstelie, Brunner, and Ardon (2000) document test score gaps and historical trends that have exacerbated these patterns. Betts, Zau, and Rice (2003) find that in San Diego racial and socioeconomic gaps in math and reading performance are very large. For instance, in spring 1998, the reading achievement of Hispanic and black students in grade 8 on average equaled or lagged slightly behind that of white students in grade 5. Although the researchers found that these gaps narrowed between 1998 and 2000, large gaps remain.

Prodded by these stubborn achievement gaps, virtually all state governments have recently implemented school accountability systems. For instance, in 1999, California implemented the Public School Accountability Act. It mandates state content standards, student testing, and a school-level accountability system that has "teeth"—that is, consequences for failing schools. This trend has gained further momentum with the passage in 2001 of the federal No Child Left Behind (NCLB) Act. NCLB requires that states test students in specific grades, to set criteria for "proficiency" and minimum percentages of students expected to meet those proficiency standards, and sets out an escalating series of interventions for schools identified as failing.

[1]The National Commission on Excellence in Education (1983).

A key component of both federal and state systems is an emphasis not only on increasing average achievement levels but on reducing the large gaps in achievement among student racial groups and socioeconomic groups.

The creation of school accountability systems represents a helpful step forward, but it has left school districts to their own devices as they find ways to boost overall achievement and to narrow the achievement gaps in their own schools. What is to be done? One might think that a simple solution is to spend more—for instance, by cutting class size or by increasing teacher salaries in hope of attracting a greater number of highly qualified individuals to the teaching profession. However, rigorous studies have found only limited evidence that such spending translates into systematically better outcomes for students.[2] Further, broad untargeted reforms such as these will do little to narrow achievement gaps. Rather, what appears to be needed is a large and focused intervention targeted at the students who lag furthest behind.

A number of large school districts in the United States have recently embarked on such reforms. Indeed, the pressure created by states' accountability systems and similar provisions under NCLB have induced most districts to struggle to find new and better ways to teach students. But at the same time, the sheer scope of the reforms in some districts sets them apart from the efforts under way in other districts. Two examples of standouts are the districts in Chicago and San Diego. The Chicago Public Schools system has received national attention for its accountability-based reforms that direct additional resources (and sanctions) toward students who fall seriously behind grade level and toward schools that serve large numbers of such students. President

---

[2]For early national evidence see the classic work by Coleman (1966), and for a fairly recent review, see Hanushek (1996). For the California context, see Betts, Rueben, and Danenberg (2000) and Betts and Danenberg (2001). Using data from San Diego, Betts, Zau, and Rice (2003) provide some evidence that class size is negatively associated with student gains in test scores, but in elementary school grades only, and that teacher qualifications are associated with gains in test scores, but mainly in higher grades. For somewhat mixed evidence on the effect of California's Class Size Reduction (CSR) program, see CSR Research Consortium (1999, 2000), Bohrnstedt and Stecher (1999, 2002) and Jepsen and Rivkin (2002).

Clinton (1998) went so far as to mention the reforms favorably in a State of the Union address.

Following on the heels of Chicago Public Schools, San Diego Unified School District (SDUSD) has recently implemented its own quite distinct flavor of reforms and, like Chicago, has garnered national attention, in part because of the sweeping nature of the reforms.

The district's ambitious "Blueprint for Student Success" represents a major redeployment of resources to assist students who lag seriously behind. Although the Blueprint reforms are now beginning to assist students whose math achievement falls behind national norms, the initial focus was squarely on reading achievement. Students who perform poorly on district reading assessments can be placed into double or triple-length English classes, some of which have reduced class sizes. These courses, which concentrate on improving students' reading and writing skills, are referred to as literacy block and literacy core. In addition, students can receive further assistance outside regular school hours and in summer school and in some cases can be held back a grade. At the same time, the district has embarked on systemic reforms to teacher training, with peer coaches being assigned to improve teaching methods, and has introduced numerous professional development offerings to help teachers sharpen their skills. Another component of the reforms includes curriculum and textbook spending to improve the classroom environment.

The reforms have received high degrees of interest locally, statewide, and nationally. The William and Flora Hewlett Foundation donated \$7.5 million dollars over the first two years of the reforms to help implement the Blueprint and another \$6 million in 2003. The Bill and Melinda Gates Foundation donated \$15 million over five years. Marshall Smith, former U.S. Under Secretary of Education and currently Program Director for Education of the Hewlett Foundation, told the *San Diego Union Tribune*: "This really is the most important urban school reform effort in the country. . . . If the reforms work here they will have a national effect because ideas travel."[3] Similarly, the Atlantic Philanthropies, based outside California, made a \$5 million grant to the

[3]McGee (2001).

district to support the Blueprint implementation. Alan Ruby, a senior official for Atlantic Philanthropies is quoted in a district press release as saying: "We believe that the reforms underway at San Diego City Schools are extraordinarily important and demonstrate that district-wide reform in an urban school district setting is possible."[4] Articles in the *San Diego Union Tribune* in October 2002 quote former U.S. Secretary of Education Rod Paige and former California Secretary of Education Kerry Mazzoni as strongly supporting the Blueprint. In addition, reforms that resemble the Blueprint are now being introduced elsewhere. For instance, in New York City, Mayor Bloomberg has implemented reforms including "literacy and math coaches" at the school level and a more uniform elementary school curriculum.[5]

Locally, the Blueprint has generated intense interest and controversy, with the business community supporting district board members and candidates for the board who support the Blueprint. However, the local teacher's union has expressed disappointment that teachers have not been involved more in the design of the reforms. In fact, a survey of district teachers conducted for the school board by the American Institutes for Research found that many teachers oppose the reforms.[6]

Perhaps most important, the Blueprint has generated diverse reactions among various ethnic/racial communities. Supporters—for example from the Urban League—express gratitude for the additional resources being targeted at low achievers and the narrowing achievement gap.[7] Detractors express a number of concerns. Alberto Ochoa, Co-Chair of the San Diego County Latino Coalition on Education, in an October 29, 2001, op-ed in the *San Diego Union Tribune* expressed concerns that it would be Latinos who would be predominantly assigned to the extra-length English classes. In a separate October 9, 2001, letter on behalf of the coalition to the district school board, Ochoa equated the

---

[4]See http://www.sandi.net/news-releases/news-releases/2002/020212.grant.html. For information on the additional Hewlett Foundation grant see http://www.hewlett.org/Programs/Education/Achievement/News/sandiegogrant.htm.

[5]Gootman (2005).

[6]American Institutes for Research (2002).

[7]See Price and Steppe (2002).

double- and triple-length English classes that the final version of the Blueprint implemented with academic tracking. He expressed concern that this tracking would reduce Latinos' ability to complete course requirements needed for admission to the University of California and California State University (UC and CSU) systems.[8] Clearly, the doubling and tripling of the length of English classes for some students raises critical issues.[9]

The charge that the district's system is merely tracking would become moot if it could be shown that the additional time devoted to literacy leads to better student outcomes. A proof in this regard would have to demonstrate that in the short run, literacy block/core and the other English classes with increased length increased the rates of improvement in English reading tests.

With the eyes of education policymakers from around the country focused on San Diego, important questions arise about the extent to which the reforms succeed in improving reading achievement. In addition to examining overall trends, it is equally if not more important to understand which components of the reforms are having the most and least beneficial effect. The only way to study these issues is to drill down to the level of the classroom and the individual student and teacher so that the package of interventions received by each student can be measured accurately.

Unfortunately, it is impossible to use existing state databases to shed much light on the mechanics of these important reforms. Although researchers have already done much useful work with these databases, the inability of the databases to measure achievement at the student level, to track students over time, to track teachers over time, and to link students to their teachers means that some of the most important education policy questions facing California and the nation cannot be addressed effectively.[10]

---

[8]See Ochoa (2001a, 2001b).

[9]See also Cuban and Usdan (2003a) for a review of the political controversy surrounding the reforms.

[10]For example, the reports by the CSR Consortium (e.g., Bohrnstedt and Stecher, 2002) that have analyzed the statewide CSR initiative have repeatedly pointed out that

Basic Objectives

For this study, we have put together an ideal dataset for addressing the Blueprint reforms: a student-level dataset that is longitudinal (i.e., it follows students over time), that links students to teachers, and that contains rich characterizations of everything from student background to curriculum, student participation in specific Blueprint programs, and teacher qualifications. This report analyzes the data statistically, providing the first student-level analysis of the effect of the Blueprint reforms. It studies the school years 1999–2000 through 2001–2002. We chose these years because the district formally introduced the Blueprint in summer 2000, with partial implementation of some components of the reform in 1999–2000.

The overall objectives of this research project are fourfold. First, we want to explore how many students participated in each intervention in the first two years. In this regard we also want to study how the district uses test scores to assign students to interventions. Second, we want to determine the effect of the Blueprint reforms on average reading achievement and on the gap in reading achievement between racial/ethnic groups and between groups defined by their socioeconomic and language status. Third, we seek to understand the mechanisms through which the Blueprint has worked most and least effectively. Our fourth goal is to provide policy advice. Each year district administrators have fine-tuned components of the reforms, and it is important for administrators to have objective evaluations of the reforms when making these policy decisions. With Superintendent Alan Bersin's departure from the district in July 2005, the Blueprint is at a crossroads. Dr. Carl A. Cohn, the new superintendent whom the district board appointed to take over in October 2005, will have many difficult choices to make about the future direction of the reforms. We believe that our findings can assist other districts statewide and nationwide as they design education reform plans of their own. Indeed, former Superintendent Bersin's appointment by the governor to become the state Secretary of

---

we cannot know the effect of CSR for sure without following individual students over time and taking account of variations in the qualifications of their teachers.

Education in July 2005 should only heighten curiosity outside San Diego about the effect of the Blueprint on student achievement.

Relation to Other Research

The American Institutes for Research was hired by the SDUSD school board to evaluate the Blueprint and has thus far published evaluations of the first two years of the Blueprint (2000–2001 and 2001–2002).[11] Roughly speaking, that research has employed two techniques. The first is to measure progress in student achievement, in SDUSD and in a number of comparison districts using several of the statewide tests. The second technique has involved surveys of district teachers.

Both of these approaches have already yielded valuable insights. The test-score comparison suggests that test scores overall have risen in SDUSD but have risen just as fast in comparison districts, if not faster. The one key advantage held by SDUSD in the first two years of the reforms is that reading scores at the elementary school level grew more quickly than in comparison districts. At the high school level the opposite was true. Math scores in SDUSD improved but at slightly slower rates than in comparison districts. Because the researchers did not observe the Blueprint interventions in which a specific student engaged, the American Institutes for Research reports are very careful to state that the Blueprint did not necessarily "cause" any of these differences in trends.[12]

It is important to understand that this "horse race" between districts cannot inform the debate on whether the Blueprint has improved achievement. After all, other districts around the state have felt the same

---

[11]See American Institutes for Research (2002) and Quick et al (2003). See also Stein, Hubbard, and Mehan (2004) for a perceptive comparison of the "cultures of reform" in SDUSD and New York City's District #2. Former SDUSD Chancellor of Instruction Tony Alvarado made major contributions to academic reforms in both districts. Hightower (2002) also provides an overview of the reforms.

[12]Similarly, the American Institutes for Research reports do use student-level test score data (for San Diego only), but because these data-points are not supplemented by information on whether the individual student participated in a given Blueprint intervention, the student-level data cannot provide much more detail than the overall districtwide trend analysis.

pressure to introduce reforms to boost achievement and to narrow the surprisingly large achievement gaps between racial, socioeconomic, and language groups that exist all across California. They too have implemented reforms. For instance, it is well known that the superintendents of SDUSD and Los Angeles Unified School District (LAUSD) have consulted with one another frequently. Some of the reforms in LAUSD bear a distinct resemblance to those in its sister district to the south. LAUSD has increased its use of Open Court for teaching reading in the elementary school grades, like San Diego has. Thus, the comparison of test-score trends across districts, although of vital importance, can tell us about the relative success of reforms in different districts, but it cannot tell us about the extent to which reform packages have succeeded in an absolute sense.

There is a second and more fundamental issue about this horse-race approach. San Diego was among the top-ranked large districts in California in 1998, the first year of the new testing regime, and it has maintained that position through recent years. However, it is unclear whether we should expect two districts that started at different test score levels to improve at the same rate. The pattern statewide has been for low-scoring schools and districts to catch up somewhat with counterparts that initially scored at a higher level. It is not clear whether this represents a genuine narrowing of the achievement gap across districts or a statistical artifact of the tests employed by the state.

The teacher surveys conducted by the American Institutes for Research are not linked to individual schools but do give an overall picture of teacher reactions in San Diego. In short, teachers on the whole express reservations about the way the reforms were implemented, including, more specifically, a lack of consultation with teachers about the design of the reforms and a concern that teachers lost some of the flexibility they previously had to design curriculum and lessons specific to their classes. For example, in its first-year survey, American Institutes for Research (2002) reports that 58 percent of teachers agreed or strongly agreed with the statement that "The Literacy Framework is helpful for designing my lessons." (The Framework is an integral part of the Blueprint, enumerating and describing various approaches that teachers should use to boost the literacy of their students.) However, 88.2

percent of teachers reported that they were "not at all" involved in the decisions about the implementation of the Blueprint. When given the statement "If I had concerns about the Blueprint, I know that the district would listen to them," 9.0 percent agreed or strongly agreed, 87.9 percent disagreed or strongly disagreed, and 3.2 percent failed to answer. When asked whether they enjoyed teaching more or less during 2000–2001 than during the previous year, 17.6 percent reported that they enjoyed it a little or a lot more, compared to 55.2 percent of teachers who reported that they enjoyed teaching less. A large majority of teachers stated that the Blueprint significantly influenced their feelings about teaching that year. One of the most useful parts of the teacher survey asked teachers about the extent to which various components of the reforms held promise. The component that teachers believed held least promise was the peer coach program that places teacher trainers inside schools to work with classroom teachers. Quick et al. (2003) report on a follow-up survey of teachers in the 2001–2002 school year that continued to find that teachers had concerns about various aspects of the Blueprint.

These survey results from the American Institutes for Research reveal that teachers have considerable misgivings about the overall Blueprint and some of its components. But, of course, these findings in no way prove that the Blueprint has failed to boost student achievement.[13]

The present report is intended to complement the existing American Institutes for Research studies. We did not conduct teacher surveys, nor did we replicate those studies' careful comparison of overall district test-score trends with trends in other districts. Rather, our goal was to examine gains in individual students' reading achievement to test

---

[13]Another noteworthy publication, edited by Hess (2005), provides an overview of the evolution of over a dozen aspects of the San Diego district and is a useful reference on the inner workings of San Diego as a major school district. It includes an update on test score trends by Margaret Raymond that matches the American Institutes for Research conclusions fairly closely and summaries of the union-administration relationship, special education, professionsal development, and a host of other issues. Zau and Betts contributed an overview of school choice in the district, and Betts provided a qualitative overview of how the Blueprint works. However, the book does not deal at all with the issue of whether and how the specific Blueprint interventions boosted student achievement.

whether participation in specific Blueprint interventions has in fact boosted reading proficiency. This student-level analysis is valuable because it gets inside the "black box" to help us better understand which Blueprint reforms have proven most successful to date. It also allows a convincing analysis of socioeconomic and racial gaps in student achievement and the extent to which the Blueprint has affected those gaps.

Design of the Report

The next chapter provides more detail on the Blueprint reforms and then outlines the set of questions we seek to answer and the analytical approach we use. Chapter 3 studies the implementation of Blueprint interventions in the first two years, documenting student participation rates in each intervention. In addition to presenting overall participation rates and rates by student subgroups, the chapter discusses whether the "right" students were assigned to interventions as determined by their reading test scores. Chapter 4 provides a statistical analysis of the extent to which Blueprint interventions have worked. Chapter 5 analyzes the cumulative two-year effect of the Blueprint on student achievement and various measures of the achievement gap. Chapter 6 explores the dynamics of the effect of the Blueprint interventions, and Chapter 7 tests for potentially adverse side effects. Chapter 8 provides an overview and a tentative discussion of policy. We say "tentative" for a simple reason: Studies of systemic education reforms have often shown that the modifications take some time to work. Implementation is rarely perfect in the first year or two, and personnel may require considerable training before the reforms truly take root. Because this report examines the first two years of the Blueprint reforms, the reader should bear this caveat in mind.

2. Overview of Blueprint Reforms, Key Policy Questions, and Research Design

We begin by describing the demographic setting of SDUSD—the host for the Blueprint reforms. As the second-largest school district in California and the eighth-largest nationally, SDUSD enrolled 141,000 students in 1999–2000, the first year of our study. The district serves a diverse population of students. For instance, in 1999–2000, non-Hispanic whites made up only 27.5 percent of students, compared to 37.2 percent for Hispanics, 16.6 percent for African Americans, 9.1 percent for Asians, 8 percent for Filipinos, and 1.6 percent for other racial/ethnic groups. In that same year, 63.2 percent of students were eligible for free or reduced-price meals, and 28.1 percent were English Learners (ELs). The district serves a considerably more disadvantaged group of students than the typical district in California, although in many respects its students resemble those in other large urban districts statewide. As a border city next to Tijuana, Mexico, San Diego also has high rates of in- and out-migration, at least among lower-income groups. To the extent that race, income, and mobility predict test scores, we see in San Diego an archetype of the sort of large urban district that will have to boost test scores markedly if it is to meet the federal mandate of "no child left behind"—that is, having all students meet state proficiency standards of achievement by the target date of 2012.[1]

Summary of Blueprint Reforms

In 1998, Superintendent Alan Bersin enlisted the help of Chancellor of Instruction Tony Alvarado to develop and implement the Blueprint.

[1]See Chapter 2 of Betts, Zau, and Rice (2003) for a more detailed comparison of SDUSD with California as a whole and with other large urban districts in the state.

Chancellor Alvarado helped to adapt some of the reading reforms that he had previously introduced as Superintendent of Community School District #2 in New York. The Blueprint that emerged in San Diego emphasizes the concept of "Balanced Literacy," which calls for teachers to promote reading "by, with, and to children." The central idea in this approach is that teachers assign to students readings at varying levels of difficulty. The teachers become more actively involved (reading with or to students) as they introduce progressively more difficult text to their students. Stein, Hubbard, and Mehan (2004) provide a fuller description.

The Blueprint consists of three main strategies that prioritize a student's literacy and mathematics abilities. The first strategy is *prevention*. This strategy applies to all students and teachers and focuses on extensive training of teachers, effective classroom materials, and enhanced teaching of students. The second strategy is *intervention*. Teachers identify below-grade-level students who then receive extra instruction through programs including extra-length English classes, extended day or summer school programs, and more focused teacher training in literacy or mathematics, depending on the students' needs. The final strategy is *retention*—that is, having a student repeat a grade with accelerated support. Contrary to many districts that focus their retention efforts at the exit grades (i.e., fifth or sixth grade for elementary school or eighth grade for middle school), the Blueprint targets the entry grades of first grade for elementary school and sixth grade for middle school (seventh grade for junior high school). Students who are still significantly below grade level despite the intervention efforts at the end of the year in these grades will be retained and placed into accelerated classes the following year.

Initially, the interventions focused on reading, although in 2000–2001, special courses in mathematics were introduced in secondary schools. Because of this focus on reading, and because of the large number of English Learners in the district who face the immediate challenge of mastering English, this report focuses on the effect of the Blueprint on reading achievement.

Although the Blueprint has a large number of strategies, the theme that unites these strategies is extra time on task for students, with a focus on the basics of reading and writing, rather than a pure focus on literature. All of this is backed by professional development for teachers that was designed to help teachers choose appropriate teaching strategies for students at various levels of literacy. However, the Blueprint is not in general prescriptive in the sense of requiring that teachers teach from specific texts at specific times.

The prevention strategies for students that were in place in the first year, 2000–2001, included

- Use of a new literacy framework in all grades, which outlines methods that teachers can use to boost literacy,
- "Enhanced classes" for all kindergarten and grade 1 teachers (which consisted of professional development, provision of highly structured Open Court teaching materials, and funds for other classroom materials),
- "Genre studies," also known as Enhanced Literacy, which consists of a two-period English class, with a focus on improving students' reading and writing skills; this class is intended for all students in the entering grade of middle or junior high school (grades 6 and 7, respectively) who are near to, at, or above grade level in their reading achievement; in addition, genre studies teachers receive related professional development, and
- One or two peer coaches for all schools to help teachers learn proven teaching methods.

With the exception of the genre studies course given to students at or above grade level in grades 6 or 7, all of the above preventive strategies are aimed at all students in a given gradespan. In addition, two other preventive strategies were directed at focus schools (the elementary schools with the weakest scores in the state test, ranking in the bottom tenth statewide). These schools received an extended school year, a second peer coach, and other funds and staff. In addition, the elementary schools that ranked in the second-lowest decile of the state ranks, known as API 2 schools, received a second peer coach and additional funds but not an extended school year. In the first year of these programs, 2000–2001, there were eight focus schools and 11 API 2 schools.[2]

The second category of Blueprint reforms is a detailed set of interventions. Unlike the preventive measures, the interventions are targeted at specific groups of students. Decisions about who receives these interventions are based upon student test results. The testing in reading is done as follows. K–3 students and grade 4 EL students are assessed individually by their teachers, and a Developmental Reading Assessment (DRA) level is determined. Students in grades 4–10 are given a test called the Stanford Diagnostic Reading Test (SDRT) in a group setting. Students who score significantly below grade level may be given another exam that is conducted by the teacher on an individual basis, to confirm the results of the group-administered test. This effectively gives students a second chance. If the student performs poorly on the second test, he or she is assigned to one of the interventions. The Blueprint lays out very specific exam score bands that determine a student's designation.[3]

Below, we outline the key intervention strategies and the grades officially covered according to the Blueprint formally adopted in 2000. In some cases, our data show that the district changed the grades covered, and the following descriptions note those exceptions:

- Genre studies/literacy block. (We will refer to this more simply as "literacy block.") Probably the best-known intervention is this variant of genre studies given to students who lag below or significantly below grade level. In grades 6 and 7 of middle and junior high school, students who are below grade level in reading

---

[2]API is the acronym for the Academic Performance Index, a statistic measuring overall student achievement in a school. The California Department of Education calculates the API for each school annually. It also ranks schools into API deciles. Hence, API 2 schools rank in the second-lowest decile of achievement statewide.

[3]For instance, students who take the SDRT are identified as belowgrade level if they are 1.1 to 3.0 grade equivalents behind norms in reading, and they are identified as significantly below grade level if they are more than 3.0 grade equivalents behind. In grade 9, students who are below or significantly below norms in reading are assigned to literacy block and literacy core classes, respectively, unless they show improved performance when they take the second test, the Analytical Reading Inventory (ARI).

attend the same sort of double-length genre studies classes as do students who are at or above grade level, but in this case class size is reduced to 20. Students in higher grades through grade 10 also receive these courses if they lag below or significantly below grade level in reading. (San Diego High School also offers literacy block in grade 11.) In addition, class size is reduced to 20 in grade 9. There is an additional option for some grades.

- Genre studies/literacy core. For students significantly below grade level in grade 9, the literacy class is extended to three periods. Again, these class sizes are 20:1. We will refer to these classes more simply as "literacy core." In 2001–2002, grade 6 and 7 students also began to participate in literacy core.
- Extended Day Reading Program (EDRP). In all schools with grades 1–9, students below and significantly below grade level in grades 3, 6, 7, 8, and 9 (beginning winter 2001 in the last case) receive three 90-minute periods each week of supervised reading before or after school. In practice, we found that EDRP was implemented in grades 1–8 in both 2000–2001 and 2001–2002.
- Summer school. The Blueprint calls for two types of summer school. The first and more novel type of summer school is aimed at students in most K–9 grades who lag below and significantly below grade level. Students are asked to attend for six weeks, for four hours per day. EL students are automatically eligible to attend this "Blueprint summer school." In addition, all secondary school students with D or F grades attend a more traditional type of summer school consisting of six weeks of courses in core subjects.[4] We will focus on the former, less-conventional type of summer school and refer to it as Blueprint summer school, reserving the term "summer school" for the more traditional sorts of makeup classes for students who have failed a specific course. Some schools in the district, mostly elementary schools, are year-round schools, which means that

[4]Summer school for kindergarten was phased in at four elementary schools in 2000–2001 and extended to all elementary schools in 2001–2002.

their schedules do not permit the implementation of Blueprint summer school. At these schools, students in affected grades who lagged behind in reading participated in special intersession studies in lieu of Blueprint summer school.

- Grade retention. In extreme cases, students may be asked to repeat a grade and are given additional support in the year that they repeat the grade. The district intends to identify students who lag seriously behind soon after they arrive at a school. Accordingly, grade retention is limited to entry-level grades of elementary and middle school/junior high school: grades 1, 6 in middle school, and 7 in junior high school.[5]

Table 2.1 provides an overview of the preventive measures and interventions in place each year. For this table, we have used our analyses of actual participation by year and grade. We have indicated that a given grade participated in a given Blueprint element if more than 0.5 percent of students participated. (In almost all cases, implementation was far above this level.) There were several cases such as EDRP in which we found that the program was implemented in more grades than originally envisioned by the Blueprint. In addition, especially at the high school level, we found that a very small percentage of students who officially were in grades beyond a given intervention actually did participate.

Key Policy Questions

This research had four overarching goals. First, we explore how many students have participated in each intervention in the first two years and whether the "right" students have participated, as determined by their reading test scores. Second, we determine the effect of the Blueprint reforms on average reading achievement and on the gap in reading achievement among various groups of students. Third, we test whether the various Blueprint elements have varied in their effectiveness. Our fourth goal is to provide policy advice, which flows primarily from our findings about the relative effectiveness of the individual Blueprint elements.

---

[5]The first time Blueprint retention decisions were made was in spring/summer 2001.

Table 2.1

Summary of Blueprint Implementation by Grade and Year

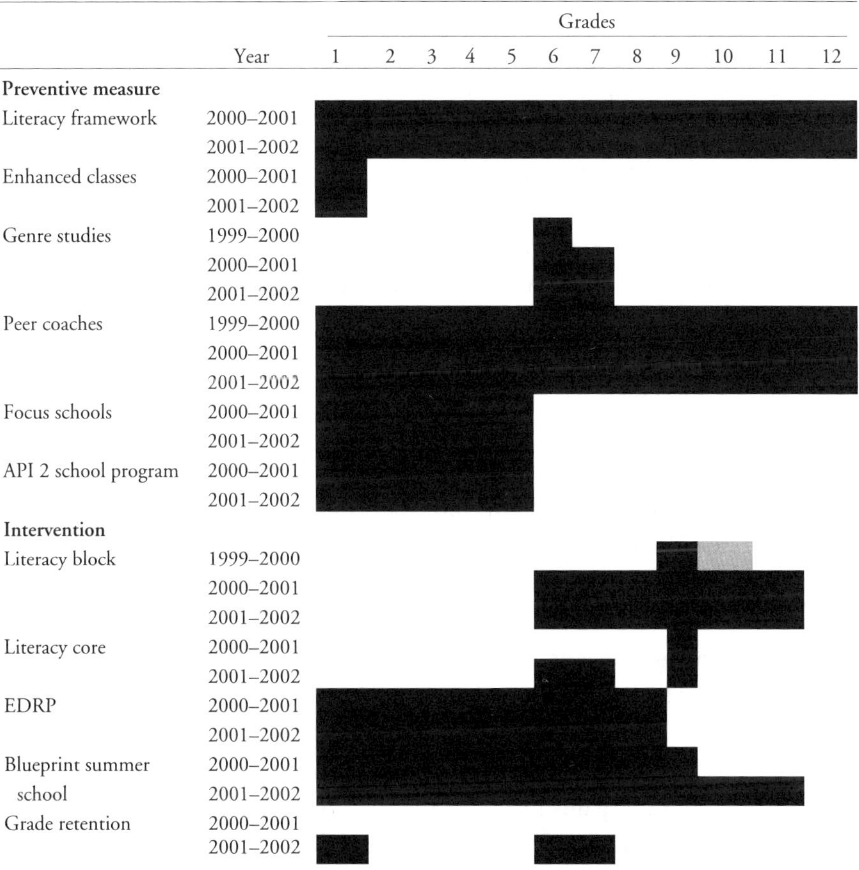

	Year	1	2	3	4	5	6	7	8	9	10	11	12
		Grades											
Preventive measure													
Literacy framework	2000–2001	■	■	■	■	■	■	■	■	■	■	■	■
	2001–2002	■	■	■	■	■	■	■	■	■	■	■	■
Enhanced classes	2000–2001	■											
	2001–2002	■											
Genre studies	1999–2000						■						
	2000–2001						■	■					
	2001–2002						■	■					
Peer coaches	1999–2000	■	■	■	■	■	■	■	■	■	■	■	■
	2000–2001	■	■	■	■	■	■	■	■	■	■	■	■
	2001–2002	■	■	■	■	■	■	■	■	■	■	■	■
Focus schools	2000–2001	■	■	■	■	■							
	2001–2002	■	■	■	■	■							
API 2 school program	2000–2001	■	■	■	■	■							
	2001–2002	■	■	■	■	■							
Intervention													
Literacy block	1999–2000									■	▒		
	2000–2001						■	■	■	■	■	■	
	2001–2002						■	■	■	■	■	■	
Literacy core	2000–2001									■			
	2001–2002						■	■		■			
EDRP	2000–2001	■	■	■	■	■	■	■	■				
	2001–2002	■	■	■	■	■	■	■	■				
Blueprint summer school	2000–2001	■	■	■	■	■	■	■	■	■			
	2001–2002	■	■	■	■	■	■	■	■	■	■	■	
Grade retention	2000–2001												
	2001–2002	■					■	■					

NOTES: Black boxes indicate implementation districtwide or nearly districtwide with more than 0.5 percent of students in the given grade having participated in a given intervention or having attended a school receiving a given preventive measure. Gray boxes indicate partial implementation in selected schools. Because of space constraints, kindergarten participation is not shown but is described in the text. Peer coaching was the one Blueprint element that was widely introduced in 1999–2000. In 1999–2000, in all grades, between 58 and 78 percent of students attended a school that had implemented the peer coach program at some level. On average, in 1999–2000, two-thirds of students attended schools with a peer coach, compared to over 95 percent of students in the later years. In 2000–2001 and 2001–2002, a few schools did not have peer coaches because of delays in hiring or turnover. Programs that do not show a row for 1999–2000 were not implemented in that year. According to documents produced at the time, EDRP was introduced on a very limited basis in 1999–2000 in grades 3, 6, 7, and 8. However, student records from that year do not report any such enrollment.

We focus in particular on the following questions:

- How widely and quickly have the various programs been implemented? How does participation vary by race, English Learner status, and parental education?
- Do the "right" students, as determined by reading test scores, receive the stipulated interventions?
- Do students who participate in the double-length literacy block classes improve their reading achievement more quickly than students who do not participate?
- Do triple-length literacy core English classes improve reading achievement more quickly than double-length classes?
- Has Extended Day Reading had a meaningful effect on reading achievement?
- Does Blueprint summer school lead to gains in achievement? If so, at what grades does it work best? For students at year-round schools that could not implement Blueprint summer school for scheduling reasons, did the substitute intersession Blueprint classes work equally well?
- Are the various Blueprint reforms reducing the achievement gap among races and between students who come from highly educated and less highly educated families?
- Have the "whole-school" reforms such as those at the focus schools, the API 2 schools, and the hiring of peer coaches led to significant gains in achievement at the affected schools?
- Can we find any evidence that the effectiveness of the various reforms varies with teacher experience? For example, did the programs at the elementary Focus schools help students with the most experienced teachers more? Similarly, in middle and high schools, did the various types of extended English classes prove more effective when taught by teachers with the most experience?[6]

---

[6]In neither case is the answer clear. More highly experienced teachers may be better placed to implement the reforms. Conversely, less-experienced teachers potentially stand to gain more from the fairly prescriptive guideliness in the Blueprint and might also be

Overview of Data Used and Research Design

This research builds on the database constructed for the first PPIC report on student achievement, *Determinants of Student Achievement: New Evidence from San Diego*, by Betts, Zau, and Rice (2003). In that report, the authors compiled longitudinal data on student records and linked those records with information on the qualifications of the teachers in each classroom. A particularly noteworthy aspect of the teacher database is that it goes considerably beyond the measures of teacher qualifications available at a school level in the state database, providing attributes such as college major and minor and detailed subject authorizations at the middle and high school levels.

We augmented this database in a number of ways—first by adding variables indicating whether students had participated in each of the specific Blueprint interventions, as well as regular summer school. Second, we augmented our student database by using district-administered measures of reading achievement to determine who was eligible to participate in specific Blueprint interventions. Third, at the school level, we added measures indicating whether elementary schools were focus schools or API 2 schools. (Recall that under the Blueprint, both types of elementary schools received additional funding or staffing.) Fourth, we added the ratio of peer coaches to enrollment at the school, to give a sense of the intensity with which the peer coach program was implemented in each school in a given year. We also added a measure of the average teaching experience of peer coaches at each school. Fifth, we updated the data to the 2001–2002 school year to provide a full picture of the effect of the Blueprint in its first two years.

We accessed numerous district databases to piece together this information for each student. For example, we worked for several months to develop accurate measures of whether a student had participated in (regular) summer school or Blueprint summer school,

more open to changing the way they teach, not having developed years of lesson plans in the way that more experienced teachers might have done.

using course codes that varied somewhat between the two years that we studied.[7]

There are three important and distinct innovations in this research relative to the more typical California school-level research that uses state Department of Education data. The first is that as a result of two years of data-cleaning, we have compiled a rich database on individual students and teachers, with extremely detailed information on both students' academic backgrounds and teachers' qualifications. This enabled us to distinguish in fine detail the effect of various prevention and intervention strategies student by student.

The second innovation is that we have multiple years of data for all students except those who have recently moved to San Diego or who have just started school. As in Betts, Zau, and Rice (2003), this allows us to take into account any unobserved but fixed characteristics of students, their neighborhoods, and their schools. The importance of this approach can hardly be overstated. Researchers have long known that students learn at different rates, often for reasons that go beyond the school itself. By comparing a student's gains in performance over as many as three years, we can "net out" variations across students in their innate rate of learning, while detecting even small effects on learning from participation in a specific Blueprint intervention in one or two years. (Because one of our three years of data is before the Blueprint was implemented, a student can participate in a given intervention for at most two years.) This is far preferable to simpler approaches that compare achievement at a point in time between two students, without first taking into account either their scores the year before or differences in their average rates of learning. In effect, each student becomes his own "comparison group" because we will test whether the student learns more in the years that he participates in a given intervention than in years in which he does not. Similarly, we control for unobserved characteristics of the student's home zip code and his school. The latter is particularly important for assessing the effect of a school's being

---

[7]For more detail on variable construction and the assignment rules for each Blueprint intervention, see Appendix A.

designated a focus or an API 2 school. We want to know whether something positive happens to student achievement in those years that a focus or API 2 school receives additional support from the district, above and beyond the pre-existing trend in student achievement at these schools.

To control for pre-existing trends in individual student's reading achievement growth, we include a year of gains (from spring 1999 to spring 2000) that precedes almost all of the Blueprint interventions and preventive measures.

3. Patterns of Student Participation in Blueprint Interventions

Introduction

This chapter examines the population and characteristics of students who participated in the Blueprint's student-specific interventions in 2000–2001 and 2001–2002. The four interventions under consideration in this chapter are the EDRP, Blueprint summer school, literacy block/core, and Blueprint-related grade retention. Excluded are the two school-level preventive programs offered at focus schools and at API 2 elementary schools. In some sense, we can think of these as schoolwide interventions. We do not include them in this chapter because the Blueprint applies these interventions school by school, and the decision to implement them is unrelated to the test scores of individual students.

Students were eligible to participate in the various interventions through two routes. First, the district used reading tests (other than the state test that we examine later in the report) to identify students who were below grade level or significantly below grade level. Students in either of these categories were recommended for one or more interventions in the following year. Second, all English Learners, who by definition have not mastered English, were eligible to participate. In the first part of the chapter, we examine the placement of EL students into interventions. In the second part, we examine the extent to which the district assigned non-EL students to interventions based on their test scores in reading.

Overall Patterns of Student Participation

Tables 3.1 through 3.4 show participation rates in the four interventions by grade and year. EDRP participation is shown in Table 3.1. The table shows that in both school years, one-quarter of students in grades 1 through 8 participated in the program. The highest rates of participation are in grades 1 to 3, above which participation tails off. Overall roughly 21,000 to 22,000 students participated in this reading program in either year. Participation in fact spans a slightly greater range of grades than in the original conception of the Blueprint.

Table 3.2 shows participation rates in Blueprint-related summer school. What is immediately obvious is that participation doubled from 2000–2001 to 2001–2002, from 11 to 22 percent. In some ways this is not surprising, because the Blueprint was introduced immediately before summer 2000, when the first Blueprint summer school sessions took place. Again participation rates decline in the higher grades, but this is largely by design, because Blueprint summer school was conceived as an intervention for students up to and including grade 9.

Table 3.3 reports the rate of Blueprint retention for students in eligible grades. The first time this intervention was used was in spring/

Table 3.1

Percentage of Students Participating in EDRP

	Year	
Grade Level	2000–2001	2001–2002
1	31.1	35.3
2	33.0	33.2
3	41.2	34.7
4	27.8	30.4
5	22.4	27.1
6	15.6	18.6
7	9.5	11.9
8	9.7	10.2
Overall	25.2	26.3

NOTE: The "overall" percentages in this chapter are calculated at the student level and, therefore, are weighted averages of the percentages in each grade, based on enrollment.

Table 3.2

Percentage of Students Participating in Blueprint-Related Summer School

	Year	
Grade Level	2000–2001	2001–2002
1	17.7	31.7
2	15.7	28.9
3	16.5	27.3
4	8.7	24.4
5	14.6	23.4
6	20.9	24.6
7	4.1	22.3
8	6.9	20.9
9	14.2	22.9
10	0.0	10.6
11	0.0	2.0
12	0.0	0.4
Overall	11.3	21.9

Table 3.3

Percentage of Students Participating in Grade Retention

	Year
Grade Level	2001–2002
1	1.3
6	0.7
7	2.8
Overall	1.3

summer 2001. The results indicate that very few students were retained for reasons mandated by the Blueprint. Retention is generally viewed by educators nationwide as a last resort, and the district's placement rules appear to adhere to that view. Of the various interventions, grade retention is the placement decision most governed by recommendations of teachers rather than by test scores alone. Indeed, state law leaves the final decision to the teacher.

Table 3.4 shows the distribution of students in different literacy courses. Literacy block and core represent interventions as opposed to

Table 3.4

Percentage of Students Participating in Literacy Placement

Grade	Single-Period	Block	Core	Genre Studies
		2000–2001		
6	4.8	36.7	0.0	58.4
7	60.2	39.8	0.0	0.0
8	68.4	31.6	0.0	0.0
9	62.3	18.0	19.6	0.0
10	65.8	33.9	0.3	0.0
11	93.5	6.5	0.0	0.0
12	99.5	0.5	0.0	0.0
Overall	64.6	25.3	3.2	6.9
		2001–2002		
6	4.8	26.2	2.6	66.4
7	63.9	34.7	1.3	0.0
8	71.6	28.2	0.1	0.0
9	65.7	18.4	15.9	0.0
10	66.1	33.4	0.5	0.0
11	97.2	2.8	0.0	0.0
12	99.9	0.1	0.0	0.0
Overall	66.6	22.3	3.2	7.9

preventive measures, because they are meant for students with low scores on a combination of standardized tests. Block consists of a daily two-period English course whereas core consists of three periods. Genre studies is another two-period English course, but it is viewed at the district level as a preventive measure aimed at students who are at or above grade level. Students in genre studies do not typically have low test scores. For completeness, we also show the percentage of students enrolled in single-period English classes of the sort that prevailed before the introduction of the Blueprint.

The results in Table 3.4 indicate that in the grades in which the block/core intervention is a possibility, just over one-quarter of students are either in literacy core or block. The flip side of this coin is that apart from grade 6, in which students at or above grade level participate in genre studies, the vast majority of students remained in regular single-period English classes. The table also indicates that, for the most part, students take literacy block and core only in the grades in which the

Blueprint states that these programs are available. There are minor exceptions. For instance, literacy block is officially offered in grades 6 through 10 (and through grade 11 at San Diego High School) but a handful of grade 12 students did enroll in block in either year, probably through joint decisions of teachers and parents. Similarly, a very small percentage of students were enrolled in a course described as literacy core outside grade 9, the principal grade for which core was designed. (The district's guidelines allow for sixth and seventh grade students to be in core as well in 2001–2002, and we observe participation consistent with this.)

Interventions as a "Package"

The next broad question we asked is whether it is more appropriate to think of these specific interventions as separate from each other or as part of a package of multiple interventions for students who are lagging behind. Table 3.5 reports on the distribution of students by the total number of interventions in which they took part.[1] In both years it was extremely rare for students to participate in three or more interventions. About two-thirds of district students did not participate in any student-level intervention. This finding demonstrates that the district targeted interventions in a quite focused way. Of those who participated in at least one intervention, two-thirds to three-quarters participated in only one intervention in a given year.

To gain further insights about the experiences of individual students, we examined the dynamics of their participation across the two years for the programs. Two policy relevant questions arise here. After a student enters a specific intervention, does he or she become "stuck" in that intervention for a second year in 2001–2002? Second, did the expansion of the Blueprint in 2001–2002 bring in new students or did it primarily expand the number of interventions experienced by the students who had already participated in at least one intervention in the prior year?

---

[1]For the purposes of tabulating these totals, we considered a student participating in either literacy block or core as having been in a single intervention. We did this because the overall strategy of these interventions is similar (double- and triple-length English classes) and because a few students switched from one to the other midyear. In this way we do not overcount student participation.

Table 3.5

Percentage of Students Overall Participating in Blueprint-Related Intervention Programs

Number of Programs	Year 2000–2001	Year 2001–2002
0	66.0	62.0
1	26.1	24.3
2	7.4	12.7
3	0.5	1.0
4	0.0	0.0

To analyze participation dynamics, we considered only those students who were in the district both years. Table 3.6 reports for each intervention the participation rates for students based on whether they participated in the first year. For example, the first panel of the table shows that of those who participated in EDRP in 2000–2001, 51.2 percent participated again in the following year.

Looking at participation dynamics across EDRP, Blueprint summer school, and block/core intervention, we find that between 38 percent and 55 percent of those students who participated in an intervention in the first year did not participate in the next. Blueprint summer school

Table 3.6

Percentage of Students Overall Participating in Individual Blueprint Interventions Between 2000–2001 and 2001–2002

EDRP		2001–2002	
		Did not participate	Participated
2000–2001	Did not participate	83.9	16.1
	Participated	48.8	51.2
Blueprint summer school		2001–2002	
		Did not Participate	Participated
2000–2001	Did not Participate	81.1	18.9
	Participated	55.2	44.8
Literacy placement (block/core)		2001–2002	
		Did not Participate	Participated
2000–2001	Did not participate	82.2	17.8
	Participated	38.2	61.8

exhibited the highest exit rates at 55 percent, whereas being in either literacy block or core had the lowest exit rate at 38 percent. Conversely, we only occasionally see students who did not participate the first year participating in the next. The highest entry rate into an intervention is with Blueprint summer school. In this case, 19 percent enter into Blueprint summer school (for the first time) the following year. This increase no doubt reflects the scaling up of summer school in summer 2001 to additional grades and schools.[2]

Although on an intervention-by-intervention basis our analysis suggests a slight trend toward students exiting from an intervention after the first year, this is not the case overall. In fact, Table 3.7 shows that more students increased their number of interventions rather than decreased them in the second year of the Blueprint. There are two explanations for this. First, participation in Blueprint summer school doubled from 2000–2001 to 2001–2002. Second, the number of possible interventions rose from three to four as the first Blueprint grade retentions were announced in spring/summer 2001.

Table 3.8 breaks down these figures further to show transitions from specific numbers of interventions from one year to the next. This table conveys the fact that students who participated in two or more interventions in the first year, who typically lagged far behind in reading, had well above a 50 percent chance of participating in fewer

Table 3.7

Percentage Change in the Number of Interventions per Student from 2000–2001 to 2001–2002

Fewer in 2001–2002	Same in 2001–2002	More in 2001–2002
14.9	64.0	21.1

[2]Another reason why it is important to look at the number of students who participate in an intervention one year but not the other is that in Chapter 4 we will model the effect of these interventions on student learning. Our main statistical model will compare the rates of gains in reading achievement for individual students in years they participated and did not participate in a given intervention. However, we build a year of "nonparticipation" into this analysis because we include a year of data from before the interventions were widely introduced.

Table 3.8

Percentage Distribution of Overall Dynamics by Number of Interventions per Year

		2001–2002				
		0	1	2	3	4
2000–2001	0	78.6	15.7	5.3	0.4	0.0
	1	36.1	38.3	23.5	2.0	0.1
	2	24.3	37.4	34.8	3.5	0.1
	3	14.4	45.0	29.7	9.9	0.9

NOTES: The numbers 0–4 represent the number of Blueprint-related interventions a student received in a given year. Because Blueprint grade retention did not begin until the 2001–2002 school year, students could at most receive three interventions in 2000–2001. Row entries do not always total to 100 percent because of rounding error.

interventions the next year. Similarly, among students who participated in only one intervention in 2000–2001, 36.1 percent did not participate at all in the following year, compared to only 25.6 percent who participated in two or more interventions.

How does this square with the results of Table 3.7 that suggested on average students were more likely to increase their participation in the second year? The answer is clearly that just over one in five students in the large group of students who participated in no interventions in 2000–2001 did participate in one or more interventions in 2001–2002.

Overall, the picture that emerges is that students who enrolled in interventions in the first year were more likely than not to exit from at least one intervention in the second year. At the same time, about a fifth of the large group of students who did not participate at all in the first year became involved in at least one intervention in the second year, as Blueprint programs such as summer school were expanded. *In other words, in the second year, on the whole, student participation increased in scope rather than in intensity.* Also, most students who participated in Blueprint interventions took part in only one of the four or five interventions available each year. It is perhaps best not to think of the interventions as a "package" from the point of view of the typical student.

Characteristics of Students Participating in Each Intervention

This section examines student characteristics to investigate how participation in the programs varies according to the students' backgrounds. Throughout this section, we present pooled data across the school years 2000–2001 and 2001–2002 to give an overall picture of participation by student characteristics during the first two years of the Blueprint.

Figure 3.1 shows the relationship between parental education and participation in EDRP and Blueprint summer school. An interesting pattern emerges. For EDRP, we see that each successively lower level of parental education is associated with a doubling of the rate of participation. Those students with parents whose highest degree is high

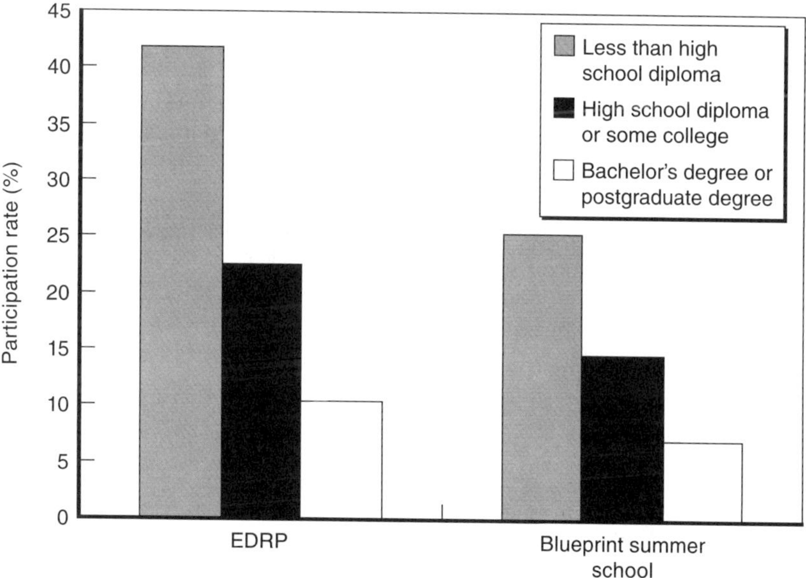

NOTE: Rates are calculated based on all students in relevant grades in either 2000–2001 or 2001–2002 and thus are an enrollment-weighted average of participation in the two years.

Figure 3.1—Student Participation Rates in the Extended Day Reading Program and Blueprint Summer School by the Level of Education of the Student's More Highly Educated Parent

school or some portion of college participate twice as much (22.6%) as those whose parents have completed college or graduate school (10.5%). Those students whose parents did not earn a high school diploma participate at double even that (41.8%). Summer school participation follows a similar pattern of participation rates, roughly doubling as parental education falls. Table 3.9 shows the underlying numbers for all five interventions and for completeness also shows genre studies, intended as a preventive measure for students who are at grade level in reading, and traditional single-period English classes. The table reveals that participation in each of Blueprint summer school, Blueprint retention, literacy block, and literacy core is strongly inversely related to parental education.[3]

Finally Tables 3.10 and 3.11 show how the rate of student participation depends on students' ethnic backgrounds and English

Table 3.9

Percentage of Students Participating in Blueprint Interventions by the Level of Education of the Student's More Highly Educated Parent

Program Intervention	Less Than High School Diploma	High School Diploma or Some College	Bachelor's Degree or Postgraduate Degree
EDRP	41.8	22.6	10.5
Blueprint summer school	25.4	14.6	7.1
Blueprint retention	3.4	1.4	0.6
Genre studies	2.7	7.6	10.6
Literacy block	42.9	24.0	11.9
Literacy core	6.7	3.0	1.3
Single-period English	47.7	65.4	76.3

NOTES: We include two types of English classes that are not Blueprint interventions, for sake of comparison. Genre studies is the preventive double-length class given to incoming middle/junior high school students who are near, at, or above grade level, and single-period English refers to a traditional (non-Blueprint) English class.

[3]A related variable is the percentage of students at a given school who are eligible for meal assistance, which is a proxy for parental income commonly used in the education literature. We found much higher Blueprint participation rates in schools serving the least-affluent families. Details are available from the authors upon request.

Table 3.10

Percentage of Students Participating in Blueprint Interventions by Student Ethnicity

Program Intervention	White	Black	Asian-PI	Hispanic	Other
EDRP	12.6	26.4	18.3	37.0	15.7
Blueprint summer school	7.0	18.6	14.3	23.2	9.7
Blueprint retention	0.2	2.4	0.5	2.0	0.7
Genre studies	12.5	5.1	7.1	4.1	10.2
Literacy block	8.9	31.0	17.1	38.7	12.0
Literacy core	0.6	4.8	2.3	5.4	0.8
Single-period English	78.0	59.0	73.5	51.8	76.9

NOTES: Asian-PI shows combined figures for Asians/Pacific Islanders. See also the notes to Table 3.9.

Table 3.11

Percentage of Students Participating in Blueprint Interventions by English Learner Status

Program Intervention	Non-EL	EL
EDRP	17.8	45.0
Blueprint summer school	11.9	29.2
Blueprint retention	0.9	2.2
Genre studies	8.9	0.8
Literacy block	18.2	49.5
Literacy core	2.0	8.7
Single-period English	70.9	41.0

NOTE: See the notes to Table 3.9.

language proficiency, respectively. All nonwhite groups participate in the Blueprint's interventions at a higher rate than do whites. Blacks participate roughly twice as often as whites do in EDRP and Blueprint summer school, and Hispanics participate at about three times the white rate. The ratios of participation relative to whites are even higher when we consider the other interventions.

Non-English Learner students are either students who are native English speakers or students whose mastery of the language suggests that they are functionally fluent. The latter are referred to as Fluent English Proficient (FEP). EL students are those who are in the process of learning English. Students not fluent in English participate two to four times as often as fluent students do in the Blueprint interventions. We had expected such a result because the district has drawn up an entirely separate set of program placement guidelines for EL students. Specifically, the district guidelines do not use SDRT scores to allocate EL students to interventions. By virtue of their language status, EL students are automatically eligible to participate in Blueprint summer school, EDRP, and literacy block.

The extremely high participation rates of EL students in all interventions apart from grade retention are an important finding. It would be wrong to claim that the Blueprint interventions affect only EL students, but they certainly are an important component of the target population.

Were the "Right" Students Assigned to Blueprint Interventions?

The analysis above gives a fairly detailed portrait of who has participated in the Blueprint reading interventions. But it tells us nothing about whether the "right" students participated in each of the interventions. Roughly speaking, for students who were not English Learners, the district used reading test scores to determine whether the students were below grade level or significantly below grade level, and assigned them to interventions accordingly. This oversimplifies the rules in several dimensions. Students who appeared to fall into either of these categories were often given a second reading test, and only if the results of this second test corroborated the initial test score were students assigned to Blueprint interventions. In addition, teachers had some say in making recommendations as to which interventions a student should enroll in. This is particularly true for Blueprint grade retention. Further, parents had the right not to enroll their children in any recommended intervention.

The main test used by the district to determine assignment to interventions is the SDRT, a norm-referenced multiple choice test.[4]

[4]The SDRT is given to students in grades 4 through 10 in the springtime. In K–3, the district instead uses the DRA, which involves a one-on-one interaction between

SDRT scores are translated into a measure called "Grade Equivalents Behind" that captures the number of grade levels a student lags behind his or her grade level. Three categories matter most to the district. The first includes students who are below grade level—a category reserved for students who are between three and one grade levels below where national norms indicate they should be. In this category students are eligible for literacy block, EDRP, and Blueprint summer school. The next category includes students who are more than three grade levels below where they should be. It is termed significantly below grade level. Being significantly below grade level makes students eligible in some grades for Blueprint retention or literacy core. All other students are either at or above grade level and are no longer specifically targeted for any one intervention.[5]

Participation Rates by Grade Equivalents Behind

As a first analysis of whether the right students participated in interventions, we can examine participation rates in each program by grade equivalents behind on the SDRT for students in relevant grades. Before examining these data, what should we expect to see? If the district is indeed using SDRT scores to assign students, students who are below the test-score cutoffs for a given intervention should have much higher participation rates than students just above the cutoff. However, participation rates for students below the SDRT cutoff for a given intervention should never be 100 percent, because the district policy is always to retest such students using a different test, to verify the need for intervention.

Table 3.12 shows participation rates among students in various grade equivalent ranges. The categories are described using mathematical notation. For instance the category "[–2,–1)" refers to students who

---

teacher and student in which the teacher assigns a reading level based on a student's reading accuracy, fluency, and comprehension of a specified set of readings. The DRA is administered three times per year, once per grading period. For placement purposes, results of these tests from one academic year are used to recommend student assignments to Blueprint interventions in the summer and academic year immediately following.

[5]Technically, these are students for whom the value of (grade equivalent – current grade) is greater than or equal to –1.0. Thus, it includes students who are only slightly behind grade level, or at or above grade level.

Table 3.12

Percentage of Students Participating in Blueprint Interventions by the Number of Grade Equivalents Behind on the Stanford Diagnostic Reading Test

	Grade Equivalents Behind or Ahead of National Norms in Reading						
	Significantly Below Grade Level			Below Grade Level		At or Above Grade Level	
Program Intervention	<–5	[–5,–4)	[–4,–3)	[–3,–2)	[–2,–1)	[–1,0)	≥ 0
EDRP	18.4	22.2	27.0	31.7	26.5	6.9	2.0
Blueprint summer school	27.3	34.1	34.5	38.4	31.6	10.1	2.8
Blueprint retention	27.3	12.1	5.2	0.0	0.0	0.0	0.0
Genre studies	0.0	0.0	0.4	0.9	2.7	12.4	16.4
Literacy block	48.4	54.6	66.5	67.5	55.7	9.6	1.3
Literacy core	23.2	21.9	11.7	1.4	0.4	0.1	0.0
Single-period English	28.4	23.6	21.4	30.2	41.2	77.8	82.3

NOTES: The column headings in this table use mathematical notation to indicate the range of grade equivalents included. For instance [–5,–4) refers to students who were strictly more than four grade equivalents behind but who were at most exactly five grade equivalents behind.

were strictly more than one grade equivalent behind and up to and including two grade equivalents behind. These are students whose SDRT scores made them just eligible to participate in EDRP, literacy block, and Blueprint summer school.

The table shows that program participation indeed varies strongly with grade equivalents behind. As should be expected based on the district's guidelines regarding test scores, there are drops in participation around the relevant cutoff points. For example, EDRP, Blueprint summer school, and literacy block participation rates all exhibit sharp drops at from [–2,–1) to [–1,0) which are the two bands surrounding the threshold score for determining if a student is below grade level or at or above grade level. Indeed, for EDRP and Blueprint summer school, participation rates rise by about 20 percentage points for students just below the test-score cutoff. Even more dramatically, participation in literacy block, the double-length English classes, rises from 9.6 percent to 55.7 percent just below the cutoff score.

There are also increases at the other cutoff that represents going from below grade level to significantly below grade level for the relevant interventions—Blueprint retention and literacy core. Participation in the grade retention program jumps from 0 percent to 5.2 percent just below the cutoff for significantly below grade level. Thus, Blueprint retention happens only to those students who are significantly below grade level, which is precisely what the rules specify. Even so, only a low percentage are Blueprint retained. At most slightly more than a quarter of students *five* grade levels behind are actually retained. We know of two reasons for this low participation rate among those so far below grade level. First, by district policy a student cannot be retained more than one grade for any reason, so some of these students were exempted for this reason. Second, some special education students were exempted because of exclusions incorporated into their Individual Education Plans.

Similarly, participation in the literacy core participation jumps from 1.4 percent to 11.7 percent just below the cutoff for significantly below grade level. Interestingly, with both EDRP and Blueprint summer school, participation rises along with better test scores for the significantly below grade level students and some below grade level students, but it then falls dramatically for those students at or above grade level.

Overall, we conclude that the district clearly uses the SDRT score cutoffs as announced, but for most interventions, students who are far below the test score cutoff are actually slightly less likely to participate than those who are just slightly below the cutoff(s). We cannot tell whether this reflects higher motivation among the students near the cutoff, greater pressure from teachers or parents to participate in the interventions when students are only slightly below grade level, or a combination of the two.

As we expected, participation in each intervention never reaches anything close to 100 percent for students who are designated below or significantly below grade level as determined by the SDRT. The main reason, as noted above, is that the district always retests such students to give them a second chance. A secondary reason is that occasionally a school is unable to provide a given intervention to a student. District officials told us that this most often happened when there were too few affected students to constitute a class (such as literacy core or EDRP). In such cases, district policy was to give additional financial resources to the school and to have the school create an alternative assistance program for the student, which was to be included in the student's Learning Contract.[6]

Perhaps more surprising is that we found a few cases in which students who were above an SDRT cutoff participated in an intervention, even though technically their performance made them exempt. District officials said that the most common reason for such decisions was that a class such as literacy core did not have quite enough students in it to be financially workable. In such a situation, a teacher could recommend that a student whom she thought was borderline should participate in the intervention.

In short, SDRT scores clearly play an important role in deciding who enrolls in specific interventions. It appears that teachers have the most leeway to keep students out of the EDRP, Blueprint summer school, and especially Blueprint grade retention, which conforms to our reading of the official district guidelines on program placement that the district provides to teachers. Literacy core also had participation rates among students with low SDRT scores that were far below 100 percent. In part this may reflect the difficulty of setting up these special classes in schools that had only a few students who were significantly below grade level. Of all the interventions, literacy block had by far the highest participation rate among students who appeared to be eligible as determined by their SDRT scores.

As a next step, we used the detailed program assignment manuals handed to school site administrators to determine the full rules for assignment of students to interventions. We used all test score results, including the secondary tests given to students who appeared to be below grade level or significantly below grade level as determined by the first test, to identify students who were eligible for each specific intervention. By eligible we mean that the student failed to score above the cutoff on

---

[6]The Learning Contract is an agreement signed by the teacher and parent(s) of at-risk students that stipulates the interventions the student will receive and potential interventions should the student's academic performance not improve sufficiently.

any of the reading tests that would exempt him or her from the intervention. In this section of the chapter we focus on non-EL students, because the assignment rules for EL students were so different and not strongly related to test scores.

As a first examination of this more complete measure of whether students are assigned properly, we calculated the ratio of the proportion of eligible students who participated in a given intervention to the proportion of ineligible students who participated. For example, a ratio of 4.3 would tell us that a student whose test scores made him eligible for EDRP was 4.3 times as likely as an ineligible student to participate in EDRP. If the ratio were 1, it would tell us that test scores were completely irrelevant in assigning students to EDRP, whereas a ratio approaching infinity would indicate that virtually no ineligible students were in fact assigned to EDRP.

Figure 3.2 shows these ratios for each intervention and year. They represent averages of all students in all grades in which a given intervention was offered. For both EDRP and Blueprint summer school, the probability of a student's enrolling approximately triples if he is eligible (as determined by test scores) compared to the case if he is not eligible. This ratio suggests that the district used test scores as reported but that many other factors also contributed to the decision to enroll. Test scores seem to have played a more decisive role in determining placement in literacy block and literacy core in both years, with the probability of participating many times higher if the student was eligible. Further, the participation ratios increased significantly in the second year of the program for both of these extended-period courses. Blueprint grade retention provides the most dramatic illustration of the use of test scores to assign students: Precisely zero of the students not eligible to be retained were retained, compared to 18.4 percent of those who were eligible.[7]

---

[7]We had to omit Blueprint retention from Figure 3.2 because the ratio of participation between eligible and ineligible students is infinity.

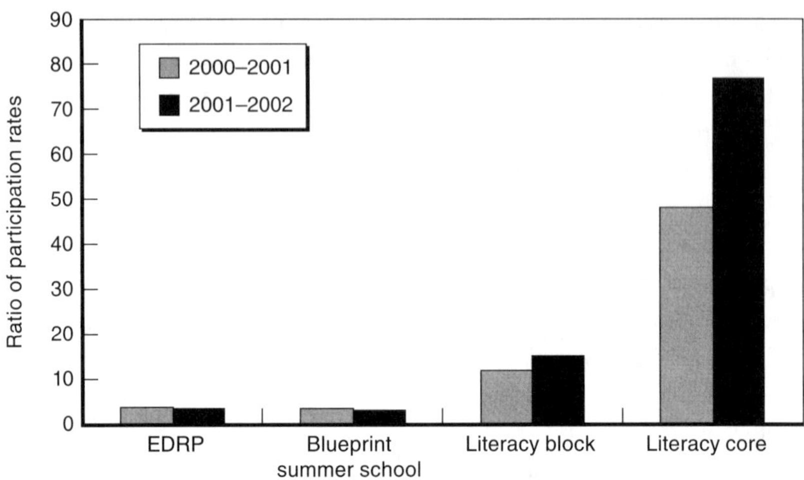

Figure 3.2—Number of Times by Which Probability of Participation Rises If Student Is Officially Eligible, by Intervention and Year

Of course, these participation ratios tell only one side of the story. We also want to know the actual percentages of eligible and ineligible students who enrolled each year. In addition, there is a third category of student—those who were initially eligible to participate in an intervention because of low test scores but who improved sufficiently on the second test given to be exempted from participation. If district staff used these test scores to assign students to interventions, we should find that participation rates were highest among those who were deemed eligible as determined by both reading tests, followed by those who initially appeared to be eligible but whose scores improved enough on a second test to exempt them, with ineligible students participating the least.

Table 3.13 shows participation rates by year for all students in the grades relevant for each intervention. For the most part, we find exactly the predicted pattern, with eligible students participating to the greatest extent and ineligible students to the least extent. For instance, in 2000–2001, EDRP participation rates were 30.7 percent, 20.0 percent, and 8.9 percent for the eligible, "initially eligible but became ineligible," and ineligible groups respectively. Clearly, test scores mattered for assignments but schools made numerous exceptions, presumably for

Table 3.13

Percentage Participation Rates by Eligibility Status, Intervention, and Year

Intervention	Year	Participation Among the Eligible	Participation Among Those Whose Scores Improved Sufficiently	Participation Among the Ineligible
EDRP	2000–2001	30.7	20.0	8.9
	2001–2002	27.4	23.5	8.3
Blueprint summer school	2000–2001	14.5	84.3	4.4
	2001–2002	30.3	59.1	10.1
Blueprint retention	2001–2002	18.4	0.0	0.0
Literacy block	2000–2001	69.0	32.2	5.9
	2001–2002	69.8	27.9	4.7
Literacy core	2000–2001	33.7	31.4	0.7
	2001–2002	61.7	14.7	0.8

NOTES: This table excludes EL students because eligibility rules are so different for them. Each cell reports the percentage participating in a given intervention out of all non-EL students in the grades that offered the intervention who fit the given eligibility status to participate.

borderline cases.[8] Teachers and parents clearly do have a say in the placement of students into Blueprint interventions.

Conclusion

This chapter demonstrates that a large minority of SDUSD students participated in reading interventions in the first two years of the program. The biggest growth in scale was Blueprint summer school, which doubled in size between summer 2000 and 2001. On the whole, students who participated in any Blueprint interventions in 2000–2001 were likely to participate to a lesser degree in 2001–2002, suggesting that

[8]One exception is Blueprint summer school in which the intermediate group, those initially eligible but whose scores rose enough to exempt them, actually participated at the highest rate. We cannot determine the reason for this anomaly, although it is worth noting that the total number of students in this intermediate category is not large compared to the eligible and ineligible pools. For instance, in 2000–2001 the 84.3 percent participation rate for those whose scores improved sufficiently to render them ineligible translated into just 291 participants out of a total of 4,168 participants in Blueprint summer school.

as their reading scores improved, they sometimes "graduated" from at least one intervention. Counterbalancing this, about a fifth of students who did not participate in any interventions in the first year of the Blueprint did participate in at least one intervention in year two, likely reflecting the expansion of services, particularly Blueprint summer school, in the second year.

Who took part in the interventions? All EL students were eligible to participate, as were non-EL students whose reading test scores suggested they were more than a grade behind in reading. Participants in the four student-based interventions that we study are much more likely to be EL. For instance, one out of two English Learners participated in literacy block on average, compared to less than one out of five fluent English-speaking students. Similarly, participants were much more likely than nonparticipants to be nonwhite or to have parents with relatively low education.

For non-EL students the criterion for eligibility was low test scores in reading. Our results suggest that the district has used test scores to assign students to interventions very much as announced. However, it would be a mistake to argue that test scores alone determine the placement of students. Test scores were most important in determining assignments to literacy block and core and least important in determining assignment to Blueprint grade retention. This matches official district policy in the sense that teachers and parents have input into assignment decisions, and this is particularly so for grade retention. It is also clear that EDRP and summer school have lower participation rates among eligible students than do literacy block and core. The most probable reason for this is that EDRP and summer school, like other interventions, are voluntary, but parents and teachers are less likely to agree that a given student should participate in these interventions that take place outside the regular school day. An additional insight from this chapter is that occasionally students who are above the official test score cutoff still participate in an intervention. According to district officials, teacher recommendations that students whose literacy skills are only marginally acceptable participate, as well as the need to fill out classes, explain this phenomenon.

4. Effect of Individual Blueprint Elements on Student Gains in Reading

Introduction

To determine which of the Blueprint's preventive measures and interventions have affected reading gains, we use regression analysis to model gains in individual students' reading scores on the Stanford 9 test.

Appendix B provides full details on the regression method used. Here, we highlight the most salient features. The first important point is that all of our models include what are known as "fixed effects" for each student, school, and zip code for the student's home residence. We do this to take fully into account the possibility that some unobserved factors related to students, schools, or neighborhoods that are fixed over time influence gains in reading achievement. The most obvious example, perhaps, is that some students, for whatever reason, learn more quickly than other students. If these "fast learners" never score low enough to participate in Blueprint interventions, whereas "slow learners" often score low enough to participate, then there will automatically be a negative relation between Blueprint participation and average gains in test scores. But this relation would not mean that Blueprint participation *caused* participants to learn more slowly. In fact, it would be exactly the opposite: Being a slow learner might cause a student to participate in a Blueprint intervention. The addition of student fixed effects solves this problem. It removes differences among students from the data. In practice, it means that we will measure the effect of participating in a Blueprint intervention by comparing reading gains for individual students in years that they participated in a given Blueprint intervention with their own gains in years when they did not participate.[1]

The use of student fixed effects raises an important question: What are the sources of variation in the data that statistically identify the effect of the Blueprint on reading achievement gains? For instance, suppose a student participated in Blueprint summer school in all years. Because the fixed effect produces the same results as if we subtracted the mean value of a student's Blueprint summer school participation from his or her participation in any given year, does this student provide us with any information about the effect of Blueprint summer school on achievement? The answer is yes. The reason is that we include in our data the reading gain between spring 1999 and spring 2000 and model this gain as a function of the student's personal and classroom characteristics during the 1999–2000 school year. *This is the year before the Blueprint was implemented.* Thus, even those students who participated in Blueprint summer school in both summer 2000 and summer 2001 provide us with information on the effect of Blueprint summer school, because we can compare their reading gains in those years with their gains in 1999–2000, the year before the Blueprint was implemented.[2]

---

[1]For a nontechnical explanation of the intuition behind fixed-effect models, see Appendix A of Betts, Zau, and Rice (2003).

[2]Three Blueprint elements were introduced in 1999–2000. The first of these, peer coaches, was introduced on a quite wide scale in 1999–2000, with about two-thirds of students in schools with a peer coach, compared to over 95 percent in the later two years. Because we model the effect of the ratio of peer coaches to total school enrollment, even for students who attended a school with peer coaching in all three years, the fixed-effect models will yield some information on the influence of peer coaching thanks to variations in this ratio. The second Blueprint element that was introduced in 1999–2000, this time on a very limited basis, was genre studies. Because genre studies classes were done only at the entry grade of middle and junior high schools, it is not possible for a student to have participated for three years in a row. So, all students with at least one genre studies course will contribute to our estimated effect of genre studies on gains in reading achievement. Similarly, a few students in grade 9 in 1999–2000 participated in a trial run of literacy block. It is theoretically possible in this case that these students re-enrolled in this program over the next two years, but in practice this did not happen. Appendix B provides more information on sources of variation after we add the student fixed effect. There, we focus on peer coaching because it was the Blueprint element that was widely in place throughout all three years of our study and therefore has a questionable amount of variation. But even here, the ratio of the standard deviation (after imposing the student

Table 4.2

School, Classroom, and Student Body Controls Used in the Statistical Models for Elementary School Students

School Characteristics
Fixed effects for each school to control for all fixed characteristics of the school.
Controls for whether the school was a year-round school
Student Body Characteristics at the School Level
Percentage eligible for free or reduced-price meal; separate controls for percentage of students who are Hispanic, black, Asian, Pacific Islander, native American; percentage of students who are EL, FEP; controls for student mobility: percentage who changed schools that year, who switched schools unexpectedly, and who were new to the district
Student Body Characteristics at the Grade Level
Mean test scores in previous spring's test of all students in the student's current grade, standardized to district average
Classroom and Teacher Characteristics
Class size; controls for teacher characteristics: interactions of credentials (intern, emergency credential, full credential) with indicators of years of teaching experience (e.g., 0–2, 3–5, 6–9); master's degree, Ph.D.; bachelor's in math, English, social science, science, language, other major (except education) (separate variables for each major); corresponding controls for minors by field except that the omitted group is teachers with a minor in education or other; the CLAD credential, (Spanish) Bilingual CLAD (BCLAD), CLAD alternative credential, BCLAD alternative credential; controls for teachers who are black, Asian, Hispanic, other nonwhite, and female

who are English Learners. BCLAD is similar but prepares bilingual teachers to teach in a bilingual classroom.

At the middle and high school levels we include all of the explanatory variables listed in Tables 4.1 and 4.2 with three modifications. First, whereas we focus on each elementary student's homeroom teacher, at the middle and high school levels we instead focus on the characteristics of each student's English classroom and English teacher. This makes sense because we are modeling gains in reading achievement.

A second modification is that at the middle school and high school levels we need to control for additional characteristics of teachers. In these gradespans, teachers can hold one or more *subject authorizations.* Subject authorizations indicate the degree of mastery of the subject matter at hand. A *teaching credential,* on the other hand, denotes mastery of more general approaches to teaching. Subject authorization levels include—in declining order of subject matter knowledge—full authorization, supplementary, board resolution, and limited assignment emergency (LAE).[6] Accordingly, we add controls for a supplementary, board resolution, or LAE subject authorization.

Third, at the middle and especially the high school level, the number of English classes that a student takes each year may vary. We therefore add indicator variables indicating that students took zero or one English course on the one hand or greater than (the normal load of) two classes in a given year.

To these models we added numerous characterizations of Blueprint elements. Peer coaches are placed in schools to interact with classroom teachers by observing their lectures and providing feedback, providing lectures while the regular teacher watches, and providing training in various other ways. We wanted to test whether the intensity of peer coaches in a school influenced reading gains. Therefore, we calculated the ratio of peer coaches to overall enrollment in the school. Our reasoning is that because class size varies little across schools in the district (Betts, Zau, and Rice, 2003), a peer coach who had to work with a greater number of classrooms could be less effective.[7] We also included the ratio of peer coach apprentices to enrollment at the school. Because a peer coach's own experience might influence his or her effectiveness, we also included a measure of the average years of teaching experience of peer coaches at the school.

At the elementary school level, two important Blueprint elements are the focus and API 2 schools, which receive substantial additional

---

[6]Full and supplementary subject authorizations are official authorizations mandated by the California Commission on Teacher Credentialing (CCTC). Board resolutions refer to decisions by the San Diego School Board to authorize a teacher to teach a specific subject, when the teacher has taken relevant college courses. These teachers may lack one or two courses required for a supplementary authorization or have enough in the general subject area but not the exact set of courses required by the CCTC. LAE authorizations are short-term authorizations for teachers with less subject knowledge. These should not be confused with an emergency credential, because LAE credentials are given to fully credentialed teachers teaching outside their normal assignment. Some high school teachers may not hold any of the above subject authorizations, because they are not yet fully credentialed teachers.

[7]We also tried simpler models that simply counted the number of peer coaches at the school. The results were qualitatively similar.

resources. We add indicator variables to indicate which elementary schools were in these groups. We note that one of the additional resources schools in both categories received was a second peer coach. Because we control separately for this, we can effectively distinguish between the effect of peer coaches, on the one hand, and, on the other, the collective effect of the other resources added through the focus and API 2 school programs.

Because we have included school fixed effects in our models, it is natural to ask how we can identify the effect of becoming a focus or API 2 school on achievement. The main answer is that we include a year of gains before the focus and API 2 preventive programs began in fall 2000. Thus, we can compare achievement growth before and after these schools were targeted to receive additional resources. In addition, some of the schools placed in one of these programs in 2000–2001 exited the program the next year by virtue of changes in the schools' API rankings, and other schools entered one of these preventive programs in 2001–2002 as their API rankings slipped. This mobility provides us with additional variation that helps to identify the effect of the programs.

The district views peer coaches and focus and API 2 schools as preventive measures. The focus and API 2 programs are in reality something of a blend of prevention and intervention because on average students at these schools have from the earliest grades been significantly behind their peers in other schools.

A final preventive measure that we control for is genre studies, the special English classes offered in the first year of middle school and junior high school for students who are not lagging behind.

Turning to pure interventions, we add controls to indicate whether students participated in the EDRP, Blueprint summer school, and at the middle and high school levels, literacy block and literacy core. In the case of year-round schools, at which it was impossible to schedule a full Blueprint summer school session, the district instead offered intersession studies, and we control for that as well. Finally, for technical reasons it was hard to distinguish between the assignment of EL students to core versus block and so we include a separate dummy variable that indicates whether the student in the given year was an EL student who participated in literacy core or block. We also include indicators for whether the student was Blueprint-retained. However, because of small numbers, we could not estimate this effect at the elementary school level. We do show results of Blueprint retention among middle school students but strongly caution that a lack of observations makes it unlikely that we could detect an effect of grade retention, negative or positive, if it truly existed.

Results

In this section we focus on models that include the set of explanatory variables listed in Tables 4.1 and 4.2 as well as the Blueprint variables. However, we tried variants that did not control for class size, that did not control for teacher characteristics, and that did not control for either class size or teacher characteristics. The results were quite similar across specifications, and so in this chapter and the next, we report on models that control for both class size and teacher characteristics. The main reason for doing this is to ensure that what on the surface may appear to be an effect of Blueprint interventions does not in fact result from schools' intentionally steering certain types of teachers toward certain types of students. The regression results showing coefficients for all Blueprint variables for all specifications can be found in the tables of Appendix B.[8]

Estimation of the models of test score gains yields coefficients that tell us the sign and size of the relationship between a given explanatory variable and gains in reading scores. But it is not enough simply to look at the sign of a coefficient to conclude whether, say, summer school boosts reading achievement. Because of random error, even if the effect were truly zero it is almost a certainty that the coefficient on summer school would not be precisely zero. Therefore, it is equally important to calculate whether the given coefficient is "significantly" different from zero. Using this approach, if we find that a Blueprint variable is statistically significant at the 1 percent level, it means that there is only

[8]Model iv from these tables is the base model for each gradespan that we will focus on in this and the next chapter. To conserve space, we do not show the host of other coefficients pertaining to student background, peers, class size, and teacher qualifications. However, for the most part our results here are very similar to those reported in Betts, Zau, and Rice (2003), who used 1998 through 2000 test score data from SDUSD.

one chance in a hundred that the true effect of that variable on gains in reading scores is zero. The standard practice in the statistical literature is to conclude that any variable significant at or below the 5 percent level is "statistically significant." Therefore we begin by showing the degree of statistical significance of each Blueprint element in a format that facilitates comparisons among elementary, middle, and high schools and then turn to the question of the size of these effects.

Table 4.3 lists the statistical significance of each Blueprint coefficient. We estimated separate models for elementary, middle, and high schools, which are shown in the three columns. The symbols "++" and "+" indicate that the given variable is significant at the 1 percent or 5 percent levels, respectively, and that the estimated effect on reading gains from an increase in the corresponding variable is positive. Similarly, the symbols "- -" and "-" indicate that the variable is estimated to be negatively related to gains in test scores, with significance levels of 1 percent and 5 percent, respectively. Blanks indicate that the given variable was not significantly different from zero for the given gradespan. Because not all Blueprint elements are provided in a given gradespan, we blacked out the corresponding boxes in Table 4.3.

The top section of the table shows the statistical significance of each preventive measure. It reveals very mixed evidence on the effect of peer coaches. The ratio of peer coaches and of peer coach apprentices to enrollment are not significant (at the 5% level) in elementary schools. At the middle school level, the peer coach apprentice variable is weakly and negatively significant, and at the high school level there is weak evidence of a negative relation between the ratio of peer coaches to enrollment and gains in reading scores. We also note that the average years of teaching experience of peer coaches does not appear to influence gains in reading test scores.

Turning to the Blueprint elements that we categorize as "preventions/ interventions," we find that the indicator variables for both focus and API 2 schools are highly significant and positive, suggesting that the flow of

Table 4.3

The Statistical Significance of Blueprint Elements in Models of Gains in Students' Reading Scores

	Gradespan		
	Elementary	Middle	High
Preventive Measure			
Peer coach as % of enrollment			-
Peer coach apprentice as % of enrollment		-	
Teaching experience of peer coaches			
Genre studies			
Prevention/Intervention			
API 2 school	++		
Focus school	++		
Intervention			
EDRP	++	+	
Blueprint summer school	++	++	++
Intersession			
Literacy block		++	--
Literacy core		++	
Literacy block/core for EL			--
Blueprint retention			

NOTES: ++ and + indicate a positive effect significant at 1 percent and 5 percent, respectively, and -- and - indicate negative effects significant at 1 percent and 5 percent, respectively. The black cells indicate preventive measures or interventions that were not provided in the given gradespan. The exception is Blueprint retention in elementary school where we lacked the number of observations to be able to estimate an effect. In addition, we caution that the lack of significance of Blueprint retention reported for middle schools could reflect lack of variation in our data. These results are based on model iv from the regressions found in Appendix B. These models condition on teacher characteristics and class size.

resources to these elementary schools has made a significant effect on reading gains. Because we have already controlled for the ratio of peer coaches to enrollment at each school, these results speak to the collective effectiveness of the other steps taken at these schools, such as the provision of additional classroom materials and, in the case of focus schools, the lengthening of the school year.

The bottom section of the table shows the estimated effects of the various Blueprint interventions. EDRP appears to have a positive and significant effect in both elementary and middle schools, although the statistical significance is higher for elementary schools. Notably, Blueprint summer school is strongly and positively significant across all three gradespans. Recall that some middle and especially elementary schools operate on a year-round schedule that is not conducive to offering summer school. In these cases, the district substituted intersession studies during the short breaks in between semesters. We could not find evidence that these intersessions affected student gains in reading achievement either negatively or positively. Blueprint grade retention occurred in small numbers in elementary and middle schools. We lacked the observations needed to estimate this effect at the elementary school level; at the middle school level, the effect was not statistically significant.

The effects of the controversial literacy block and literacy core classes offered in middle and high schools to students who are below grade level or significantly below grade level appear to have differed greatly between middle and high schools. Both courses are associated with positive gains in reading achievement (at the 1% level) in middle schools. In high schools, on the other hand, literacy block has a significantly negative estimated effect, as does our combined measure of block/core participation for EL students. Literacy core was not significantly related to gains in reading achievement.

Comparing the Effect of Peer Coaches on Students Whose Teachers Vary in Experience

It seems natural to conjecture that peer coaches might matter more or less depending on whether an elementary school student has a relatively inexperienced or experienced homeroom teacher. Although we have no data on how peer coaches allocate their time, they might devote more effort to helping fledgling teachers. Similarly, novice teachers might be more in need of assistance and more open to assistance than their more experienced counterparts. On the other hand, a more experienced classroom teacher might be better equipped to implement teaching techniques passed on by peer coaches. At the middle and high school levels, we can make the same arguments, this time about the teaching experience of the English teacher teaching a specific student.

Similarly, it seems quite possible that the value added to a student's reading achievement by Blueprint interventions such as literacy core and block, EDRP, and so on might vary depending on the experience level of the teacher. Accordingly, we interacted our various measures of peer coaching with the years of experience of the student's teacher. We did this in two phases. We first interacted teacher experience with the Blueprint elements that directly affected that teacher's classroom (peer coach intensity divided by enrollment, literacy block, and core in middle and high schools, and focus and API 2 in elementary schools). In a second model, we also included interactions between teacher experience and Blueprint interventions that occurred outside that teacher's classroom. These included Blueprint summer school or intersession and EDRP.[9]

The results were surprisingly uniform: Typically, we could find no variation in the effect of Blueprint elements with respect to the teaching experience of a student's teacher. There were some minor exceptions. At the elementary school level, EDRP was less effective (at the 1% level) if a student's homeroom teacher had 0–2 years of experience. Conversely, the API 2 interventions were estimated to be slightly more effective for teachers with 6–9 years of experience (relative to more experienced teachers). At the middle school level, the only significant result was that Blueprint summer school was associated with slightly lower gains if the English teacher the preceding year had 0–2 years of experience. At the high school level, the only significant result was also that Blueprint summer school was associated with lower gains if the English teacher the preceding year had 0–2 years of experience.

Overall, given that the vast majority of teacher experience interactions were not statistically significant, the wisest conclusion appears to be that teacher experience did not influence the effect of the Blueprint elements in systematic ways.

---

[9]In these models, we interacted Blueprint variables indicating teachers with experience of 0–2, 3–5, and 6–9 years, with the omitted group being teachers with 10 or more years of experience. The models appear in columns v and vi of the tables in Appendix B.

Blueprint Effects on Gains in Reading Achievement

It is important to go beyond the question of "which Blueprint elements had a statistically significant" effect to study the size of these effects. Our first assessment simulates the predicted effect of participating in a given Blueprint element by dividing the predicted gain in test scores by the average annual gain in test scores we observe for all students in the same gradespan. In the period under study, average annual gains in reading achievement for individual students were 25.7 points in elementary schools, 14.7 points in middle schools, and 3.3 points in high schools. These refer to gains in the reading "scaled scores." So, for example, if participating in a specific Blueprint option in elementary school is predicted to boost reading scores by 5 points, we would estimate the predicted percentage gain by dividing 5 by the average gain of 25.7, yielding a predicted gain in achievement of 19.5 percent.

We note that the gains in reading scores tail off considerably in the higher grades, a pattern seen throughout California. Because the test scores are scaled psychometrically in an attempt to ensure that a gain of 5 points means the same absolute gain in achievement anywhere on the scale, the implication is that most gains in reading achievement occur in the earlier grades. A practical implication for our simulations is that at the high school level, it takes very little to produce an eye-popping change in achievement gains. For instance, a predicted gain of 3.3 points represents a 100 percent increase in the average annual gain in reading achievement at the high school level. But at the elementary school level, a predicted gain of the same amount represents a boost in the average reading gains of only (3.3/25.7)100% = 12.8%.

Figure 4.1 shows for each Blueprint element that was statistically significant the predicted effects on average gains in reading achievement. The figure refers to our results for elementary schools. Students at both the API 2 and especially the focus schools appear to have increased their annual reading gains significantly once their schools were assigned these designations in fall 2000 or fall 2001. The predicted increases—14.6 and 34.4 percent, respectively—are very large. Because we have already

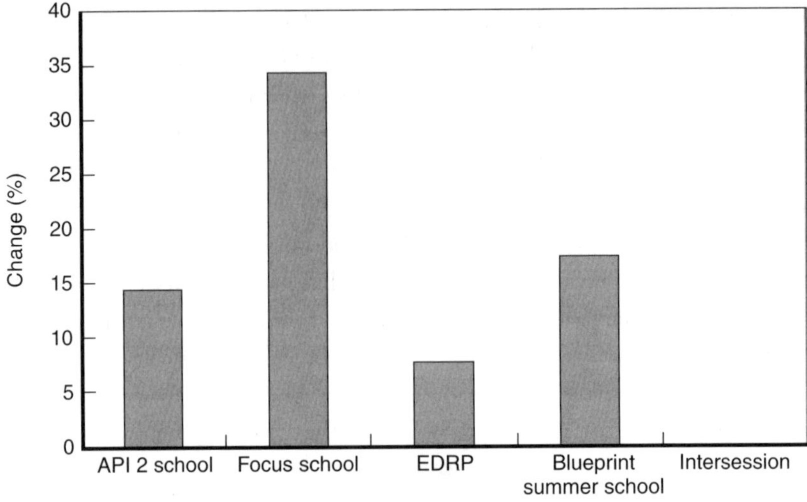

NOTES: A bar with a height of zero indicates no statistically significant effect. See Table 4.3 for a full list of insignificant Blueprint elements.

Figure 4.1—Predicted Effect of Blueprint Elements on Annual Gain in Reading Achievement Among Elementary School Students

controlled for the presence of one or more peer coaches in each school, the predicted gains at these elementary schools must stem from reform factors beyond the presence of peer coaches alone, such as the longer school year in focus schools and the additional classroom resources made available at both types of schools.[10]

---

[10]One possibility here is simply that schools in the bottom two deciles of the state rankings always show more improvement, because there is more room to grow. We are quite certain that this does not account for these impressive gains, for a number of reasons. First, our inclusion of fixed effects for each student and for each school removes differences in the average level of achievement of students at these schools compared to the level for students at other schools. Rather, it is the change in the status of a student's school that drives our results. Second, we estimated a similar model but which additionally adds dummy variables that indicate whether the given school was in API deciles 3 through 9 in each of the three years. We found that the coefficients on focus and API 2 schools were far larger than the coefficients for the third and fourth decile schools. Moreover, gains in test scores in focus and API 2 schools were significantly higher than for top-performing decile 10 schools, while decile 3 and 4 schools showed gains that were not significantly different from gains in decile 10 schools. In sum, the lack of a smooth trend suggests that focus and API 2 schools experienced gains far above

The figure also shows that the EDRP and Blueprint summer school programs are associated with appreciable gains in learning, but, as reported above, we could not find a statistically significant effect of participation in intersession studies—the analogue to Blueprint summer school available in year-round schools. We signal this lack of significance by setting the height of the corresponding box in the figure to zero.

Figure 4.2 shows results for middle schools. Again, EDRP and Blueprint summer school are associated with meaningful gains in learning in middle schools, although in percentage terms the effect of Blueprint summer school appears to be bigger at the elementary school

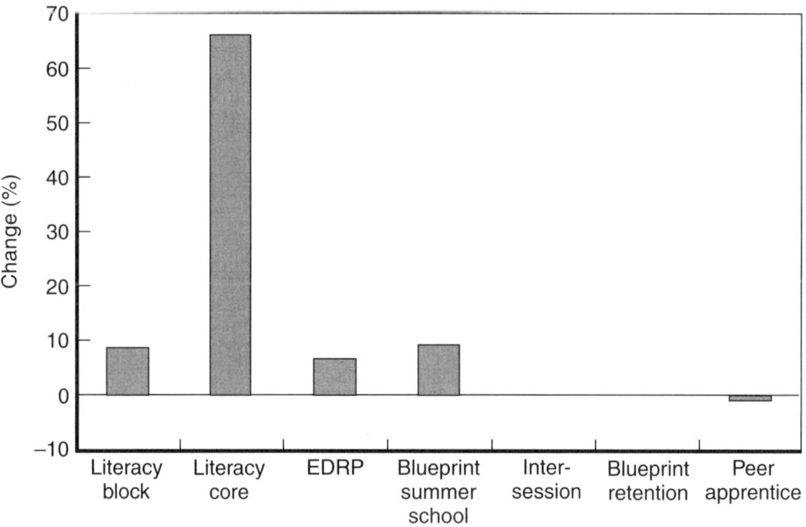

NOTES: A bar with a height of zero indicates no statistically significant effect. See Table 4.3 for a full list of insignificant Blueprint elements. For peer apprentice coaches as a percentage of enrollment, we simulated the effect of changing from zero to the mean number of peer apprentice coaches (as a percentage of enrollment). The lack of significance of Blueprint retention reported for middle schools could reflect lack of variation in our data.

Figure 4.2—Predicted Effect of Blueprint Elements on Annual Gain in Reading Achievement Among Middle School Students

---

those at similar schools that ranked just slightly higher but which did not receive additional resources.

level. The figure also shows large predicted effects on gains in reading associated with participation in literacy block and especially literacy core, the double- and triple-length English classes given to students deemed below and significantly below grade level. The predicted effect of literacy core classes—a 72 percent increase in the annual gain—is particularly large. Finally, the figure shows the predicted effect of moving from a school with no peer apprentice coaches to one with the mean number of peer apprentice coaches (as a percentage of enrollment). Although statistically significant, the size of the predicted effect is very small.

Figure 4.3 shows the high school results. These results, apart from one important similarity, differ substantially from the middle school results. The similarity is that again Blueprint summer school is predicted to lead to meaningful increases in learning. In high school, these effects

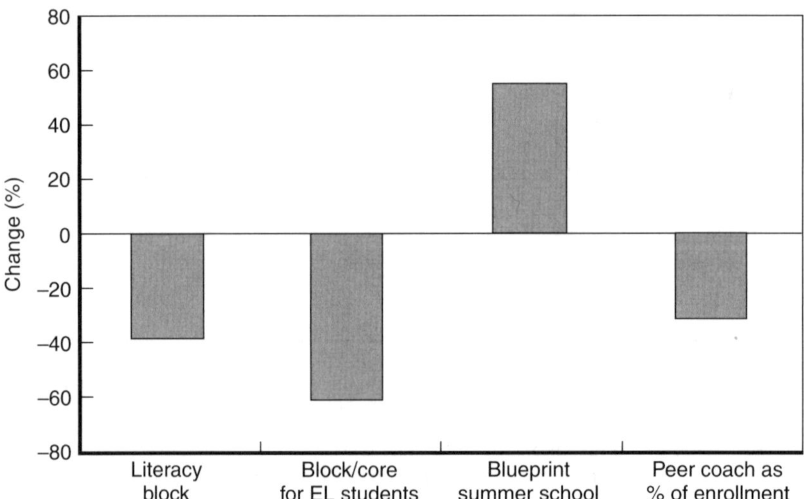

NOTES: See Table 4.3 for a full list of insignificant Blueprint elements. For peer coaches as a percentage of enrollment, we simulated the effect of changing from zero to the mean percentage of peer coaches. Because the variable "Block/core for EL students" was measured for EL students only, the predicted effect on gains in reading achievement was calculated relative to EL high school students' average annual gains—6.54 points, compared to 3.3 points for the overall population.

Figure 4.3—Predicted Effect of Blueprint Elements on Annual Gain in Reading Achievement Among High School Students

are very large in percentage terms, but as we warned above, the large percentage effect largely reflects the small average gains in reading achievement in high schools. When we compare the predicted gains in scaled scores accruing to Blueprint summer school participants, we find gains of 4.5, 1.5, and 1.8 points at elementary, middle, and high schools, respectively. As we saw above, the other Blueprint elements that were significant at the high school level were all negative. Figure 4.3 shows some fairly large predicted reductions in average rates of learning for each of these Blueprint elements.[11] Again, we need to recall that large percentage reductions in the annual gains in achievement at the high school level are not large in an absolute sense compared to the gains in lower grades.

A Tentative Cost-Benefit Comparison of EDRP, Blueprint Summer School/Intersession, and Peer Coaching

A full cost-benefit analysis of the various Blueprint interventions was beyond the scope of this initial report. Nonetheless, it is useful to compare the EDRP, Blueprint summer school, and intersession programs, for they share the basic idea of having a teacher spend extra time with lagging students outside the normal school day or school year. Recall that intersession programs are the counterpart of Blueprint summer school for students at elementary and middle schools that operate year-round. We could find no evidence that intersession studies increased annual gains in reading achievement, in contrast to Blueprint summer school. We cannot tell from our data what made intersession less productive than summer school, although we can imagine that having several short periods of study in between regular semesters might not have been as efficient as summer school that took place over several consecutive weeks. Given a shorter time period, the curriculum may not have had an opportunity to be effective either. Certainly ways should be found to boost the effectiveness of intersession studies.

---

[11]Because the EL literacy core/block variable pertains to English Learners only, we divided the predicted effect by the average gain in reading scores among EL students in high schools—about 6.5 points per year.

It is possible to create a very crude cost-benefit comparison between EDRP and Blueprint summer school. EDRP consisted of three sessions per week of teacher-supervised reading sessions, each approximately 90 minutes in length, over a 25-week period, for a total of about 110 hours of instruction. Blueprint summer school, in contrast, lasts six weeks and involves four hours of study per day, for a total of 120 hours.

Although the two programs involved approximately as much time per student, summer school involves additional costs such as transportation, administrative time, and student materials that do not apply to the EDRP, which operated at the start or end of regular school days. Indeed, American Institutes for Research (2002, p. III-7) reports that in 2000–2001, Blueprint summer school and intersession programs cost $18.3 million, or 31.8 percent of the total Blueprint budget of $57.5 million. In contrast, the Extended Day program, which at the time consisted solely of EDRP, cost $3.9 million or 6.7 percent of the overall Blueprint budget. So summer school/intersession cost the district 4.7 times as much as Extended Day.

To have been equally cost-effective as Extended Day, summer school/intersession should have contributed 4.7 times as much as did EDRP to average student test score growth. If we take the predicted percentage effect on rates of learning from Figures 4.1 through 4.3, and multiply by the average percentage of students participating in 2000–2001 using data from Tables 3.1 and 3.2, we obtain an estimate of the average effect of each Blueprint element on all students. When we take the ratio of these effects between Blueprint summer school/intersession and EDRP, we obtain estimates of 1.0 and 1.3 for elementary and middle schools, respectively.[12] In other words, summer school/intersession had about the same average effect as EDRP in

[12]For example, in elementary schools, average participation rates in 2001 were 31.1 percent for EDRP and 14.6 percent for Blueprint summer school. Multiplying the predicted effects on learning (gains of 8.0 and 17.6 percent, respectively) by these participation shares, we find average effects of 2.5 and 2.6 percent for EDRP and summer school. This yields a ratio (of summer school to EDRP effect) of 1.04 or about about 1. (Numbers in this footnote have been rounded.) Because intersession was never statistically significant, we consider its effect zero and so implicitly conclude that the combined effect of summer school/intersession is the same as the effect of summer school itself.

elementary schools and about a 30 percent bigger effect in middle schools. Both of these ratios are far less than the cost ratio of 4.7. Overall, given the cost estimates for 2000–2001, we infer that EDRP was substantially more cost-effective than Blueprint summer school/ intersession.

Obviously, there are some important qualifications that we need to make here. These rough calculations in no way say that summer school has been a bad investment. Rather, they state that EDRP has been relatively *more* cost-effective. Second, Blueprint summer school was offered in high schools, unlike EDRP, and part of the higher cost of Blueprint summer school, perhaps up to one-third, has no counterpart in the EDRP. Clearly, though, even an overstatement of elementary and middle school summer school and intersession costs by this amount would still leave the summer school to EDRP cost ratio at about 3, well above the ratio of estimated effectiveness between the two programs.

Overall, the tentative conclusion seems to be that although Blueprint summer school might be a very cost-effective reform, EDRP is more cost-effective.

We found some evidence that by 2001, the peer coach program was starting to have an effect in elementary schools, but we typically found no overall effect or slightly negative effects in elementary and higher gradespans. Yet the American Institutes for Research (2002) report suggests that the peer coach program cost $13.0 million in 2000–2001, amounting to 22.6 percent of the Blueprint budget. Although we emphasize again that a finding of "no effect" after two years should not be interpreted to mean that a given Blueprint element will *never* work, it is nonetheless striking that EDRP has been cut back substantially from its first year incarnation, when it cost less than a third as much as the peer coach program while affecting reading achievement to a greater extent.

Conclusion

It is important to bear in mind that the official launch of the Blueprint for Student Success was in summer 2000, when the first students attended Blueprint summer school, and that our analysis models gains in reading achievement from spring 2000 through spring 2002.

With only two years of data for most Blueprint elements (genre studies, literacy block, and peer coaches were phased in on a very limited basis in 1999–2000), it is certainly possible that we lack enough data to detect effects of the reforms. This seems most likely for Blueprint grade retention, which began on a very small scale in the last year of our sample.

With this warning in mind, it is quite remarkable how many of our Blueprint variables proved to be highly statistically significant. The data suggest that the Blueprint may have had both positive and negative effects in its first two years.

The effect of peer coaches is typically not statistically significant, and in a few cases may have been weakly negative. Peer coach experience did not seem to affect the effect of the peer coach to enrollment ratio.

In contrast, the funneling of targeted resources toward focus and API 2 elementary schools beginning in fall 2000 appears to have had a positive and highly significant effect. Similarly, EDRP and Blueprint summer school both are positive and statistically significant in each of the gradespans in which they are offered. The special double- and triple-length English classes, when compared to regular single-period English classes, seem to have had quite different effects at the middle and high school levels. At the middle school level, we could detect no effect of genre studies (the preventive double-length English classes that are sometimes referred to as Enhanced Literacy) but both literacy block and core were very strongly associated with gains in reading achievement. At the high school level, in contrast, literacy block for non-EL students, and block/core as a whole for EL students, were strongly associated with smaller reading gains, and literacy core was not statistically different from single-period English classes.

For the most part, we found that the estimated effect of these Blueprint variables did not depend on the teacher's experience.

Another way to look at these patterns of significance is by gradespan. On the whole, the Blueprint elements are strongly associated with gains in reading achievement at the elementary and middle school levels. At the high school level, only Blueprint summer school appears to have had a statistically significant and positive influence. Overall, the literacy block/core program is associated with reduced gains in reading achievement at the high school level.

Establishing statistical significance is important, but it leaves unanswered the question: "Has the effect of the Blueprint been large or small?" We examined the effect of participating in various Blueprint elements in terms of the percentage change in the average annual achievement gain among students in each of the three gradespans (elementary, middle, and high schools). Many of the Blueprint interventions appear to have boosted annual gains in reading achievement by 5 or 10 percent, and some Blueprint elements had effects much larger than this. For example, students at schools that were designated for additional support as a focus school exhibited an increase in annual reading gains of about one-third after this preventive program was put in place. At the middle school level, the small number of students participating in literacy core experienced a boost of about two-thirds of the average annual gains in reading achievement. At the high school level, all of the statistically significant Blueprint interventions, regardless of whether their effect was positive or negative, were predicted to change gains by roughly a quarter to a half. However, because both in San Diego and statewide, annual gains in reading scores are progressively smaller in the higher grades, the high school effects, both positive and negative, although large in percentage terms, are not especially large in absolute terms.

In sum, the results suggest that the Blueprint elements had significant and predominantly positive effects in middle and especially elementary schools. At the high school level, the effects were both positive and negative.

Although a full-scale cost-benefit analysis of the various interventions was not possible for this study, a rough comparison of EDRP and Blueprint summer school/intersession suggests that EDRP's price-tag was just over a fifth as much as for the latter interventions in 2000–2001 yet yielded comparable or only slightly smaller returns in terms of average units of test-score improvement districtwide. EDRP seems to be the more cost-effective reform.

5. Cumulative Effect of the Blueprint on Gains in Reading

Introduction

Although it is very useful to see the relative effects of each intervention, as shown in the last chapter, we still have no indication of the overall effect within the district on individual students, who may have participated in zero, one, or more Blueprint interventions or preventive strategies per year. In this chapter, we assess the overall effect of the Blueprint's elements using three measures that combine the regression estimates from Chapter 4 with students' actual participation patterns over the two-year period from summer 2000 through spring 2002. Together, the three analyses in this chapter provide important insights into the overall size of the Blueprint effects on a cumulative two-year basis. We also examine the related question of the extent to which the Blueprint altered the achievement gap among students based on language status, parental education, and race/ethnicity over the same period.

In the first method, we examine how the reading scores of participants in Blueprint interventions are predicted to have moved as a percentage of the variation in achievement in their given grade at the end of the 2001–2002 school year.[1] The second analysis also uses participation patterns of individual students and measures how this participation has affected students' test-score rankings within the district. The third method uses the estimated effects on reading gains for each

[1]The measure of variation we use is the standard deviation of test scores within the given grade. Note also that throughout this chapter we will frequently refer to "predicted" effects or "estimated" effects of the Blueprint. We say this because although we know the actual exposure of each student to each Blueprint element, we have only statistical *estimates* of the effect of each element on student reading gains.

student to estimate the cumulative two-year effect of the Blueprint on preexisting gaps in achievement related to language status, parental education, and race.

The Cumulative Effect of Size of Participation in the Blueprint

The overall effect of the Blueprint on the performance of students depends on both the size of the predicted effects as well as the rate of student participation. Accordingly, we studied the program participation of all students who in fall 2000 were in grades 3, 6, and 9, and who by spring 2002 were typically in grades 4, 7, and 10. We chose these three grades because they are the lowest grades in their respective gradespans for which a prior year test score is available. We follow students' participation patterns as they travel through their gradespan from summer 2000 through spring 2002. Using these participation patterns and the estimated effects of each Blueprint element, we were able to estimate the cumulative effect of student participation in the Blueprint.

Next, we needed to find a benchmark against which to compare these effects. Our first analysis compares the predicted change in test scores from students' actual Blueprint participation to the standard deviation in test scores in spring 2002 for all students in the given grade.[2] This produces what is known as an "effect size."

Table 5.1 shows the overall results for the three cohorts. The figures in the first column focus on students who participated in any Blueprint intervention from summer 2000 through spring 2002.[3] The table shows

---

[2]The standard deviation is a measure of variation. For the normal distribution, which has the famous bell curve shape, about 68 percent of the observations would lie within one standard deviation above or below the mean. Thus, a standard deviation improvement in test scores would be very big. A good rule of thumb is that any policy that affects an outcome by a tenth of a standard deviation or more is quite large.

[3]Because the peer coach program is designed as a preventive measure that is intended for all schools, we did not count as a Blueprint participant a student who had merely attended a school with one or more peer coaches. Rather, we defined as a Blueprint participant anybody who had participated in EDRP, Blueprint summer school, literacy core or literacy block, or had been Blueprint-retained. However, once we had identified Blueprint participants, we estimated the total effect of the Blueprint on them by including the predicted effects of having peer coaching in their schools, in the cases where the effects were statistically significant.

Table 5.1

Predicted Effect of Blueprint on Participants and All Students as a Percentage of the Standard Deviation in Reading Scores in Spring 2002

Two-Year Simulation for Students Initially in:	Average Effects for Students Who Participated in at Least One Blueprint Intervention	Average Effects for All Students
Elementary school (grade 3)	22.8	13.6
Middle school (grade 6)	5.3	2.6
High school (grade 9)	–11.0	–8.0

that elementary school participants on average are predicted to have moved up 23 percent of one standard deviation by spring 2002. This is a very sizeable improvement. In middle schools, participants in Blueprint interventions are predicted to have moved up a still substantial 5 percent of one standard deviation. At the high school level, where most of the significant interventions had negative effects, Blueprint participation is predicted to have lowered students' reading scores by 11 percent of one standard deviation.

A second issue is the effect of the Blueprint on the average student across the whole district. For this, we summed the predicted effects on Blueprint participants, as defined above, added the effect of peer coaching on the remainder of students, and divided by the total number of students. The second column in Table 5.1 shows the results. For the average student in grade 3 in fall 2000, the net effect of the Blueprint was to move him or her up 14 percent of a standard deviation. For the grade 6 and 9 analyses, the corresponding figures were a gain of 3 percent and a loss of 8 percent. There are two reasons for the smaller effects when we calculate over the entire school population rather than focusing on participants alone. More obviously, in the second panel, we are averaging out the effect of Blueprint interventions for the subsample of students who participated over a wider number of students, many of whom did not participate in Blueprint interventions. This quite mechanically lowers the average effect. More subtly, at the middle and high school levels, we did find some evidence of a negative link between peer coach or apprentice peer coach to enrollment percentages. These effects are predicted to have influenced all students in a grade regardless of whether they participated in a Blueprint intervention.

Returning to those who actually participated in at least one Blueprint intervention, the next logical question is which interventions mattered most? We know from previous chapters the participation rates in individual interventions and from the preceding section the size of the effects of each intervention. But we need to pull together *both* of these elements to work out the net contributions made by each Blueprint element. Table 5.2 shows these decompositions.

At the elementary school level, the focus schools and the summer school program appear to have the greatest effect, followed by EDRP and

Table 5.2

Decomposition of Predicted Two-Year Effect of Blueprint Elements on Participants as a Percentage of the Standard Deviation in Reading Scores in Spring 2002

Variable	Effect
Elementary school (grade 3)	
Focus school	7.1
API 2 school	3.2
Blueprint summer school	7.1
EDRP	5.4
Total	22.8
Middle school (grade 6)	
Literacy block	1.8
Literacy core	0.3
EDRP	1.5
Blueprint summer school	3.0
Peer coach apprentice	–1.3
Total	5.3
High school (grade 9)	
Literacy block	–2.3
Blueprint summer school	2.9
Peer coach	–6.1
Block/core for EL students	–5.4
Total	–11.0

the API 2 school reforms. At the middle school level, Blueprint summer school was by far the most important contributor, following by literacy block and EDRP. Literacy core contributed less, in spite of its huge percentage effect on reading gains illustrated above, simply because relatively few students enrolled in literacy core. Finally, the "Peer coach apprentice" variable is associated with a small decrease in test scores.

At the high school level, most of the Blueprint effects are negative, with the exception of Blueprint summer school. It is notable that across all three gradespans, the net effect of Blueprint summer school has been to move Blueprint participants up by about 3–7 percent of one standard deviation. Because this effect is calculated for all students who ever participated in *any* Blueprint intervention and divided by the total number of "Blueprint participant" students in the grade, this figure understates considerably the effect on students who specifically participated in Blueprint summer school.

Estimating the Effect of the Blueprint on Participating Students' Overall Ranking in the Achievement Distribution

Our second analysis examines how Blueprint participants move across the student test score rankings in their grades as a result of the Blueprint interventions. We use exactly the same approach as above, identifying students who participated in any Blueprint intervention between summer 2000 and spring 2002 and then calculating the predicted effects of the Blueprint on their test scores. But now, instead of dividing the predicted effects on test scores by the standard deviation, we examine where students would have ranked if the Blueprint had not been in place. Accordingly, we began by calculating 10 deciles, with decile 1 representing the bottom tenth of actual test scores in spring 2002 in the given grade and decile 10 the highest. We plot the actual distribution of Blueprint participants across these 10 deciles in spring 2002, at the end of our study period, and then show which decile they would have been in had they not participated in the Blueprint interventions (and had not attended schools with peer coaches).[4]

Figure 5.1 shows the results for elementary schools. The lighter bars show the actual distribution of Blueprint participants' test scores in spring 2002. As we would expect, given that the Blueprint targets interventions at students who lag behind, about three-quarters of these students rank in the bottom five deciles of reading test scores in spring 2002 when they were in grade 4.[5] The darker bars show what the distribution of Blueprint participants would have been had they not participated in Blueprint interventions.

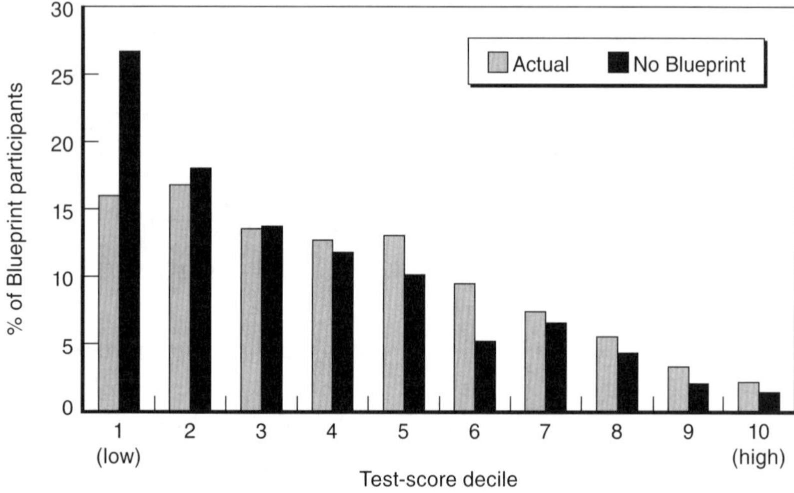

Figure 5.1—Distribution of Fall 2000 Grade 3 Blueprint Participants by Spring 2002 Test-Score Decile: Actual and Simulated Distribution Without Blueprint

---

[4]For the latter simulated distribution, we recalculate the test scores needed to be in each decile based on predicted scores.

[5]It may seem surprising that there are any students at all in the top half of the district test-score rankings. But recall that we are studying the determinants of reading scores on the Stanford 9 test; different tests are used by teachers to assign students to Blueprint interventions. Also, we are examining student achievement two years after the Blueprint began, which allows students time to move up in their relative performance.

The differences are startling. The figure suggests that with the Blueprint, 15.0 percent of Blueprint participants ended up in the bottom decile of reading by spring 2002 but that in the absence of the Blueprint fully 25.7 percent of these students would have been relegated to the bottom decile. Without the Blueprint, the share of Blueprint participants would have also risen slightly in deciles two and three and fallen across the seven highest deciles. In other words, the existence of the Blueprint appears to have boosted some of the lowest-scoring students in the district into each of the seven highest deciles of achievement. The entire distribution has shifted.

Figure 5.2 shows corresponding results for middle schools. In this case, the Blueprint appears to have shifted roughly 4.2 percent of students from the two lowest deciles into higher deciles. The interventions also appear to have shifted a smaller percentage of students from the fourth decile into a higher decile. Conversely, in Figure 5.3 the by now familiar perverse findings for high school manifest themselves. In this case, had the Blueprint not existed, it apparently would have

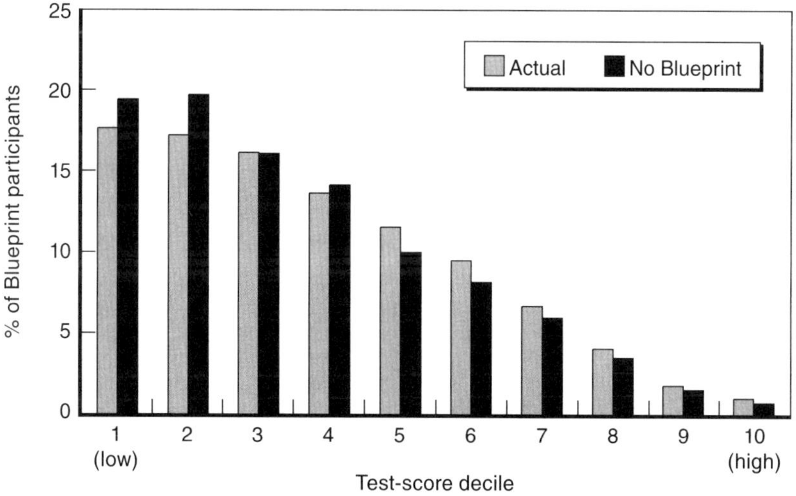

Figure 5.2—Distribution of Fall 2000 Grade 6 Blueprint Participants by Spring 2002 Test-Score Decile: Actual and Simulated Distribution Without Blueprint

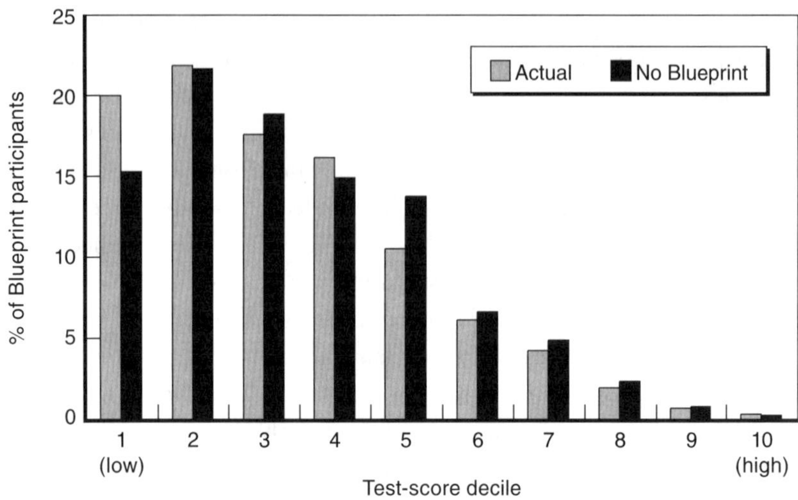

Figure 5.3—Distribution of Fall 2000 Grade 9 Blueprint Participants by Spring 2002 Test-Score Decile: Actual and Simulated Distribution Without Blueprint

reduced the share of Blueprint participants in the bottom decile by roughly 5 percent and increased their share in most of the higher deciles.

A closely related way to gauge the effect of the Blueprint is to ask by how much the typical Blueprint participant moved in the district test score rankings. For this analysis we use percentiles, which refer to the percentage of students who rank below the given student in the given grade. Actual participation rates show that participants gained 4.8 percentile points in elementary school, gained 2.3 percentile points in middle schools, and lost 1.6 percentile points in high school as a result of participation in Blueprint activities over two years.

The Effect of the Blueprint on Achievement Gaps

The final analysis focuses on various achievement gaps in reading. The groups we compare are EL versus non-EL students, blacks and Hispanics versus whites, and students with less highly educated parents versus students with at least one parent who has pursued graduate study.[6] As in the earlier analyses in this chapter, we focus on students in grades 3, 6, and 9 in fall 2000 and estimate the extent to which the preexisting gaps in reading achievement have been influenced by the various Blueprint elements over a two-year period.

Table 5.3 provides some perspective by showing the grade equivalent of students in each group and grade level in spring 2000 on the Stanford 9 reading test. These grade equivalents are derived from a nationally representative "norming" sample. Because students take the test near the end of the school year, a student who was on target in, say, grade 8, might be at a reading level of roughly 8.8. A student with a grade equivalent of 6.8 would be about two years behind national norms. The rightmost panel in the table then calculates the gap in grade equivalents between the top-scoring group of students and the other groups. For instance, we see that in grade 2 in 2000, non-EL students scored at a grade equivalent of 3.2, compared to only 2.3 for EL students. The gap, 0.8 grade equivalents, suggests that on average, EL students near the end of grade 2 are reading almost one year behind their counterparts who are fluent in English.

Comparison of the achievement gaps related to language, race, and parental education shows that the gaps are quite large as early as grade 2 and that the gaps tend to grow, peaking typically around grade 9. The largest gap observed is in grade 8, between students whose parents have some postgraduate study (after the bachelor's degree) and students whose parents did not finish high school. Here, the gap is 6.9 grade equivalents, with the former students reading near the level of a high school graduate and the latter reading at the level of a student beginning grade 6.

---

[6]Here we focus on gaps between whites and blacks and Hispanics, rather than on the white-Asian gap. Although it is true that Asian students in the district generally lag behind white students in reading, the gap is very small compared to the black-white and Hispanic-white gaps. See Chapter 4 of Betts, Zau, and Rice (2003) for evidence.

Table 5.3

Spring 2000 Gaps in Reading Achievement Between Various Student Subgroups, in Stanford 9 Scaled Scores and in Grade Equivalents

Gaps Based on Language Acquisition			
	Grade Equivalents, 2000		
Grade	Non-EL	EL	Gap
2	3.2	2.3	0.9
3	3.8	2.5	1.3
4	4.4	2.8	1.6
5	5.4	3.3	2.1
6	6.7	3.6	3.1
7	7.4	4.1	3.3
8	8.6	4.8	3.8
9	9.4	5.3	4.1
10	9.9	5.6	4.3
11	10.5	6.3	4.2

Table 5.3 (continued)

Gaps Based on Race					
	Grade Equivalents, 2000			Gap	
Grade	White	Black	Hispanic	White-Black	White-Hispanic
2	3.6	2.7	2.4	0.9	1.2
3	4.3	3.1	2.7	1.2	1.6
4	5.2	3.5	3.1	1.7	2.1
5	6.9	4.3	3.7	2.6	3.2
6	7.5	5.0	4.3	2.5	3.2
7	8.8	5.9	5.2	2.9	3.6
8	9.9	7.1	6.6	2.8	3.3
9	12.6	7.4	7.2	5.2	5.4
10	12.9	7.9	7.7	5.0	5.2
11	12.9	8.3	8.2	4.6	4.7

Table 5.3 (continued)

	Gaps Based on Parental Education								
	Grade Equivalents, 2000					Gap, Postgraduate Minus:			
Grade	Less Than High School Diploma	High School Diploma	Some College	Bachelor's Degree	Postgraduate Study	Less Than High School Diploma	High School Diploma	Some College	Bachelor's Degree
2	2.3	2.7	3.1	3.5	3.9	1.6	1.2	0.8	0.4
3	2.6	3.2	3.7	4.2	4.9	2.3	1.7	1.2	0.7
4	2.9	3.6	4.2	4.9	6.1	3.2	2.5	1.9	1.2
5	3.5	4.4	5.2	6.0	7.5	4.0	3.1	2.3	1.5
6	4.0	5.1	6.3	7.1	8.4	4.4	3.3	2.1	1.3
7	4.8	6.0	7.3	7.7	9.7	4.9	3.7	2.4	2.0
8	6.0	7.2	8.2	9.0	12.9	6.9	5.7	4.7	3.9
9	7.0	7.6	9.1	9.6	12.9	5.9	5.3	3.8	3.3
10	7.3	8.2	9.6	10.0	12.9	5.6	4.7	3.3	2.9
11	7.7	8.6	9.9	10.5	12.9	5.2	4.3	3.0	2.4

Although these test score gaps are big, they are quite typical of what we see nationally. See for instance Jencks and Phillips (1998) for a summary of the black-white achievement gap at the national level. Moreover, Betts, Zau, and Rice (2003), who studied test score trends in SDUSD between 1998 and 2000, document that achievement gaps in the district were even larger in 1998 than they were in 2000.

Given these various dimensions of the achievement gap, what has been the contribution of the various elements of the Blueprint to reducing these inequalities? Again, we examine the estimated effect of Blueprint elements that were statistically significant by examining the experience of every student in our three cohorts over two years. We calculate the predicted change in test scores resulting from participation in the various Blueprint interventions and exposure to peer coaches and compare it to the initial 2000 achievement gaps. Figures 5.4 through 5.6 show the predicted reductions in the initial test score gaps related to language, race, and parental education, respectively.

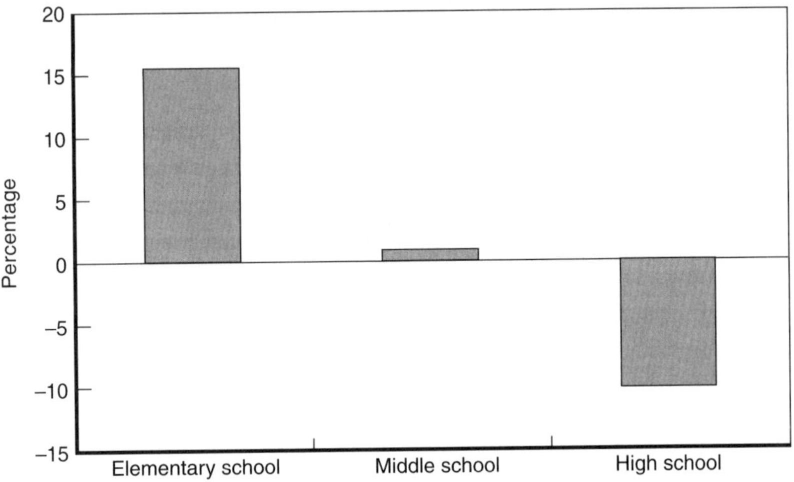

NOTE: The figure shows the predicted two-year reduction in test-score gap between spring 2000 and spring 2002 for students in grades 3, 6, and 9 in fall 2000. A positive/negative bar indicates that the initial gap is predicted to have narrowed/widened as a result of the Blueprint.

Figure 5.4—Two-Year Reduction in EL/Non-EL Test-Score Gaps Attributable to the Blueprint

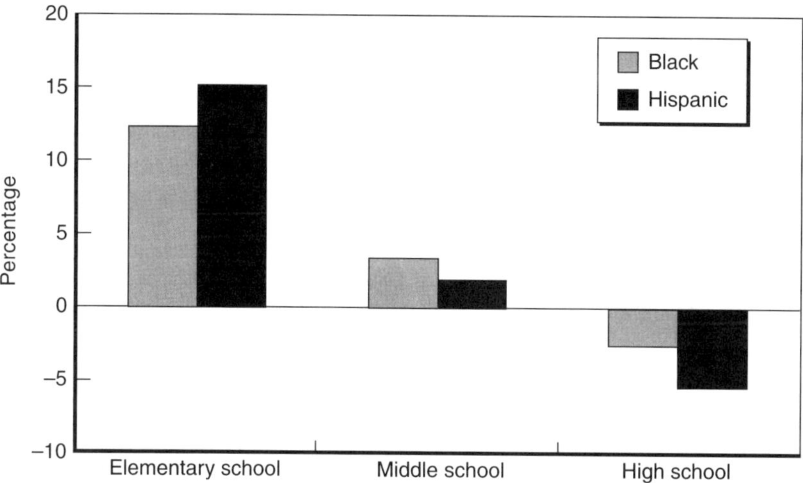

NOTE: The figure shows the predicted two-year reduction in test-score gap between spring 2000 and spring 2002 for students in grades 3, 6, and 9 in fall 2000. A positive/negative bar indicates that the initial gap is predicted to have narrowed/widened as a result of the Blueprint.

Figure 5.5—Two-Year Reduction in Test-Score Gaps (Relative to Whites) Attributable to the Blueprint

In elementary schools, all three methods of grouping students suggest that the Blueprint has led to quite substantial reductions in the achievement gap in elementary schools. Most impressive in this regard were the EL/non-EL gap, the Hispanic/white gap, and the gap between students whose more highly educated parent was a high school dropout and students who had at least one parent who continued studies beyond the bachelor's degree level. Each of these gaps is estimated to have shrunk by about 15 percent over two years because of the effect of the Blueprint.

Middle school results similarly suggest that the Blueprint reduced the various achievement gaps, but by less than 5 percent. High school results are uniformly negative in that they suggest that the Blueprint widened achievement gaps. The most dramatic instance was the high school EL/non-EL gap, which is predicted to have widened by roughly 10 percent. This mainly reflects the large negative predicted effects of literacy block and core for EL students reported in the last chapter.

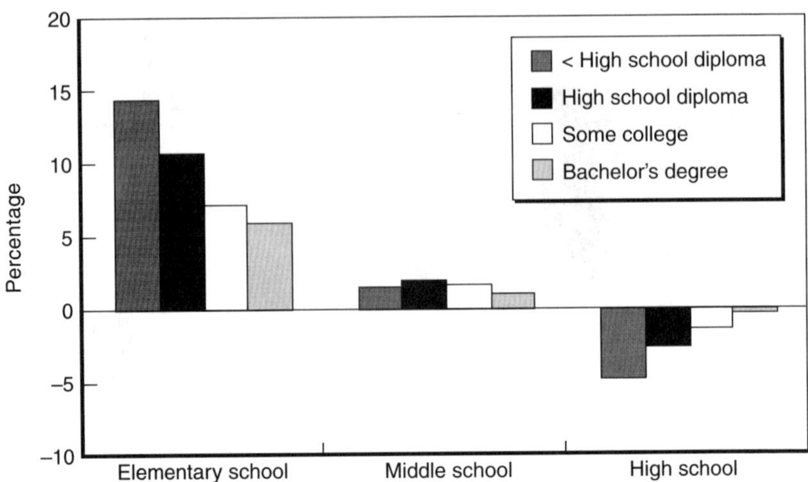

NOTE: The figure shows the predicted two-year reduction in test-score gap between spring 2000 and spring 2002 for students in grades 3, 6, and 9 in fall 2000. A positive/ negative bar indicates that the initial gap is predicted to have narrowed/ widened as a result of the Blueprint. The comparison group is students whose more highly educated parent had completed some postgraduate education.

Figure 5.6—Two-Year Reduction in Test-Score Gaps Related to Parental Education Attributable to the Blueprint

Although the effects of literacy core for non-EL students and literacy block/core for EL students were both negative, the *relative* magnitude of the predicted effects played a role in widening the achievement gap. The predicted effect of literacy block/core for EL students was much more negative, contributing to the result that is seen.

It is important to acknowledge that our estimates have assumed that the effect of each Blueprint element has been constant across student groups. Our estimates of changes in the gap therefore derive from different participation rates in Blueprint interventions among various student groups. The one major exception is that we have estimated the effect of literacy core and block on EL students separately from non-EL students. Although we devoted considerable time to testing for differences in Blueprint effects among the three sorts of groupings of students used in this chapter, we found that with two years of data, we lacked the number of observations needed to test convincingly for such differences. Indeed, when we ran models that allowed effects to vary either by race, language status, or parental education, the vast majority of cases revealed no significant differences. In addition, models estimated separately by group typically failed to find statistically significant effects of Blueprint elements, which clearly reflected our relatively small subsamples.

Thus, our assumption of identical effects among groups is likely to produce a fairly accurate estimate of the effect of the Blueprint on achievement gaps. But future work with additional years of data may allow us reliably to detect variations in the effect of specific interventions on different groups of students, which could alter our conclusions somewhat.

Conclusion

Overall, the cumulative two-year effects of the various Blueprint elements have been quite large. The reforms appear to have boosted test scores substantially in elementary schools, boosted them moderately in middle schools, and if anything, depressed reading achievement in high schools.

With the major exception of high school, then, we conclude that the Blueprint reforms have meaningfully increased gains in reading. They have done so by boosting the average achievement of those who participated and by "rescuing" students from the bottom 20 percent of the test score distribution and moving them into higher deciles. That said, the lack of similar effects in high school is notable.

We found similar patterns when we examined achievement gaps in San Diego that relate to language status, race, and parental education. Overall, the Blueprint appears to have reduced fairly dramatically the achievement gaps in elementary schools, to have reduced the achievement gap in middle schools by far more modest amounts, and to have exacerbated the achievement gap in high schools, typically to a modest degree. These conclusions apply to all three ways in which we grouped students.

In sum, we find generally positive effects of the Blueprint overall on student achievement and in terms of reducing achievement gaps, with high schools proving a major exception. We cannot say for certain why the Blueprint reforms appear to have varied so greatly in their effect across gradespans. Clearly, one reason for the relative success of the Blueprint at the elementary school level has been the package of reforms implemented at focus and API 2 schools. As for the lack of success of the Blueprint overall at the high school level, literacy core and block do not seem to have had the same positive effects we detected in middle schools.

A general explanation for the declining effect of the reforms in higher gradespans could be that in elementary schools, where teachers typically spend most of the school day with the same students, teachers have the time to learn the strengths and weaknesses of each student in reading, and tailor "Balanced Literacy" for each student appropriately. This one-on-one contact diminishes markedly at the high school level. Another possibility, which we discuss further in the concluding chapter, is that the District #2 reforms from New York did not include a high school component, so that we might expect less initial success in SDUSD in implementing the reforms at the high school level because of a lack of historical precedent. A third possibility is that high school English teachers, who typically come to class prepared to teach literature, were not as focused on basic literacy skills as were homeroom elementary school teachers. A fourth possibility is that the double- and triple-length English classes backfired at the high school level because students in that age group felt negatively stigmatized by these pullout classes, in a way that did not occur with younger middle school students. Indeed, it is quite remarkable that at the high school level, summer school classes seemed to benefit students whereas extra-length high school classes during the regular school year seemed not to prove beneficial to students. Pullout classes during the school year, because they occurred in full view of all of the students' peers, might have stigmatized students to a greater degree than the relatively secluded summer school classes. On a related note, the high school pullout classes may have damaged student morale because they could quite literally see the courses in other subjects that they were "missing out on" by looking at their counterparts who were not asked to participate by virtue of their better reading scores.

6. Testing for Variations by Year in the Effectiveness of the Blueprint

Introduction

Our analysis has examined test score gains in the school years 1999–2000 through 2001–2002. With the official introduction of the Blueprint in summer 2000, a good question is whether the effect of the various Blueprint elements varied by year. The most obvious pattern would be that as the districts' teachers and administrators gained experience with the Blueprint, this learning by doing might have increased the effectiveness of individual parts of the Blueprint. It is less likely, but still conceivable, that interventions might have become less effective over time, perhaps because of unobserved actions by any parents, teachers, students, or administrators who opposed the Blueprint. To test these ideas, this chapter repeats the analysis of Chapter 4 and allows the effect of each intervention to vary by year.

A closely related issue is whether the average effect of an intervention depended on whether a student enrolled in that intervention for one or two years. We examine this as well.

Variations over Time in Blueprint Effects on Reading Achievement

Figures 6.1 through 6.3 show the predicted effects of each Blueprint element that was significant, once we allow each effect to vary by year. Our approach was to estimate a "main" effect for 2001–2002, the last year of our study, and to add interactions to test for variations from this main effect in earlier years. Most Blueprint interventions and preventive strategies were in place for only two years, 2000–2001 and 2001–2002.

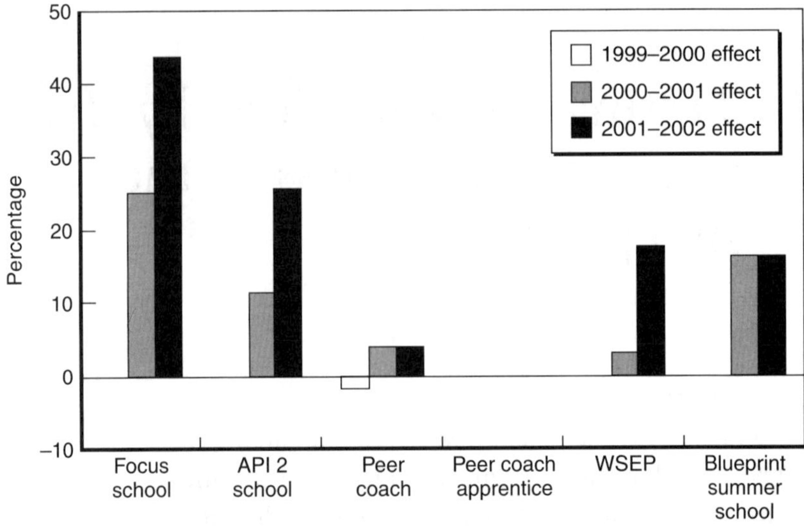

NOTES: In general, the lack of a bar for 1999–2000 indicates that the program was not in effect in that year. The only programs that we measure in 1999–2000 are the two types of peer coaches.

Figure 6.1—Predicted Effect of Blueprint Elements on Annual Gains in Reading Achievement Among Elementary School Students by Year

A few, such as peer coaching and genre studies, were implemented on a very limited basis in 1999–2000 as well, in which case we added interactions to test for variations in the effect of these elements between 1999–2000 and the base year of 2001–2002.[1]

In the figures, we present a bar showing the predicted effect of a given Blueprint element for any year in which, overall, the effect was statistically significant. In cases in which we found a significant main effect for 2001–2002 and no significant difference in an earlier year, we set the overall effect in the earlier year to the main effect. We did this so

[1]As shown in Table 2.1, literacy block was also implemented on a very limited basis in grade 9 in 1999–2000. However, we were not able to estimate a separate effect of literacy block for this year because of small sample size.

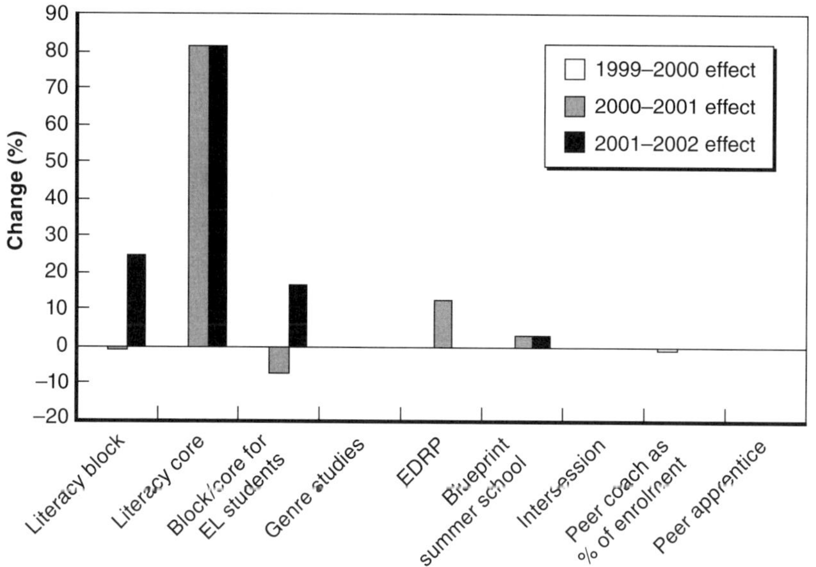

NOTES: In general, the lack of a bar for 1999–2000 indicates that the program was not in effect in that year. The only programs that we measure in 1999–2000 are the two types of peer coaches and genre studies.

Figure 6.2—Predicted Effect of Blueprint Elements on Annual Gains in Reading Achievement Among Middle School Students by Year

that readers would not read too much into small variations across years that are not statistically meaningful.[2]

Figure 6.1 shows effects by year in elementary schools. If the effect of a Blueprint element varies across years, typically the effect increases in the later years. In some cases, these increases in effectiveness are quite dramatic. For example, the estimated effect of EDRP rises from a 2.9 percent boost to the average growth in reading achievement in

[2]In the rare case in which the main effect was not significant but the interaction for an earlier year was significant, we tested that the overall effect for that year, given by the sum, was significant. If so, we used the sum of the main and interaction coefficients to estimate the overall effect for the earlier year. Otherwise, we set the effect for that earlier year to zero. Note also that by showing identical bars for years where we could find no significant difference, we present the "main" 2001–2002 effect. While minimizing in this way the chance that we are reading "too much" into variations by year, our graphs in some cases consequently suggest overall effects that do not reflect the true overall effects presented in Chapter 4.

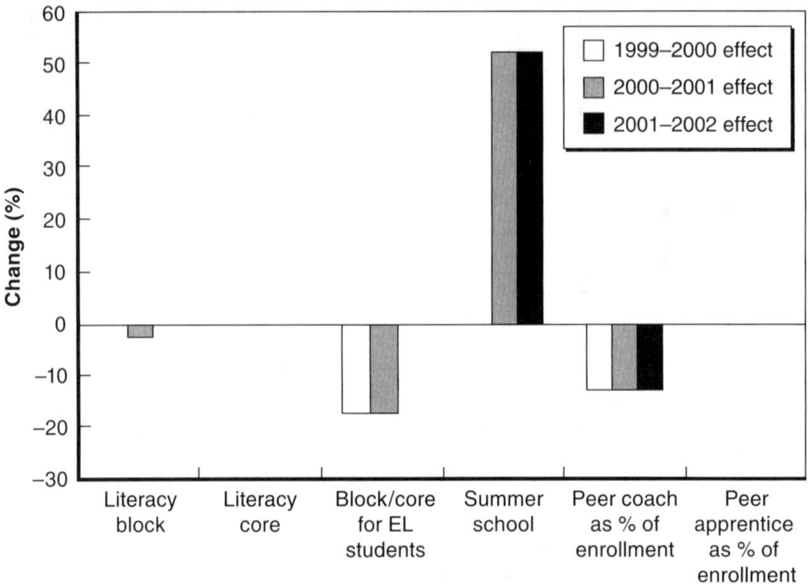

NOTES: In general, the lack of a bar for 1999–2000 indicates that the program was not in effect in that year. The only programs that we measure in 1999–2000 are the two types of peer coaches and literacy block.

Figure 6.3—Predicted Effect of Blueprint Elements on Annual Gains in Reading Achievement Among High School Students by Year

2000–2001 to a 17.7 percent boost in 2001–2002. Similarly, the effect of attending a focus school or an API 2 school rises from 25.2 percent to 43.9 percent, and from 11.3 percent to 25.8 percent, respectively. More subtly, peer coaches as a percentage of enrollment, which was not statistically significant overall, is negative in 1999–2000 and positive in the two later years and in all cases was significant. This provides some preliminary evidence that perhaps the effect of having peer coaches in the school has become more positive with time.

Results for middle and high schools, shown in Figures 6.2 and 6.3, are not as clear cut. The results for middle schools suggest that literacy block and core and peer coaches may have become slightly more effective over time, but EDRP appears to have been effective only in 2000–2001.

At the high school level, we find some evidence that the overall negative effects of literacy block and block/core for EL students may have disappeared by 2001–2002. On the other hand, the positive effect of summer school and the negative estimated effect of peer coaching did not seem to vary over time.

Variations in the Effectiveness of Blueprint Interventions Depending on Whether a Student Enrolled for One or More Years

Our main models assume that there are no positive or negative interactions between interventions within a year or across years. One reviewer asked whether a given intervention might be more effective if accompanied by another intervention in the same year or preceded by the same or a second intervention in a prior year. As Chapter 3 shows, of students who participated in at least one intervention in a given year, a strong majority participated in only one intervention, which prevents us from performing a meaningful test for interactions among different interventions with these first two years of data.

However, as a first step toward addressing the question of possible interactions between enrolling in a specific intervention for more than one year, we re-estimated the models described in the previous section to test the idea that enrolling in a specific intervention for more than one year could matter. Theoretically, the effect of enrolling in an intervention for more than one year could go in either direction. Basic economic theory suggests that holding other "inputs" constant, increasing one input more and more will eventually lead to diminishing returns, that is, a decrease in the effectiveness of a given intervention. Similarly, there is the possibility that students who stayed in a given intervention two years did not get much out of the intervention but were persuaded to stay by teachers who remained concerned about their reading ability. Conversely, it is conceivable that it takes two years of involvement with a given intervention for the student to really take off, which suggests the opposite of diminishing returns.

There is a second reason for testing whether the effect of interventions and preventive programs differed if a student participated for more than one year. Chapters 4 and 5 document very large positive effects of the focus school and API 2 school preventive programs. It is possible that these represent what are known as Hawthorne effects. This refers to a phenomenon in which any change to an organization leads to better outcomes simply because in the short run people are inspired by a change, in particular, by being singled out for additional attention. However, such effects are typically very transient and do not represent a permanent improvement. By testing students who are in focus or API 2 school programs for two years in a row, we can test whether the average effect is less than if their school had participated in either program for just one year. If so, it would provide some evidence of a temporary and essentially meaningless Hawthorne effect. Such concerns in fact apply equally to all of the student-based interventions as well.

To allow for such effects across all interventions and preventive programs, in addition to allowing the effect of enrolling in, for example, EDRP, in 2000–2001 to differ from the effect of enrolling in 2001–2002, we also allowed the average annual effect of EDRP to differ for students who enrolled in EDRP in both 2000–2001 and 2001–2002. For each intervention, we added indicator variables to indicate every possible combination of participation over time. We then explicitly tested whether the effect of enrolling in a given intervention in any particular pattern produced bigger effects than enrolling in 2000–2001 only. We reproduced the above results that the effect of enrolling in an intervention did often vary by year of enrollment. However, in all but one case, there was no additional benefit or detriment for those who enrolled in a specific intervention for more than one year. The exception was literacy block among middle school students: Students who enrolled in this intervention in both 2000–2001 and 2001–2002 had slightly higher average effects in terms of reading gains than students who enrolled only in 2000–2001 or only in 2001–2002. Put differently, this positive interaction is above and beyond the result that, in general, enrolling in literacy block in 2001–2002 was more effective than taking it in 2000–2001 only.

All in all, we found little evidence that students who enrolled in a given intervention for two or more years gained more or less per year of intervention than students who enrolled for one year only. This also provides evidence against the hypothesis that the large benefits produced at focus and API 2 elementary schools were merely transient Hawthorne effects.

Conclusion

Overall, this chapter suggests that the effect of the Blueprint's elements has increased over time, most strongly in elementary schools and to a lesser extent in middle and high schools. The evidence implies that as the district has gained experience with the various reforms, the reforms have on the whole become more effective. This is important to remember, especially for cases in which our overall analyses in Chapter 4 suggested that a Blueprint element had no significant effect on reading gains. Although it may be true that on average the given element has had no effect, over time it appears to have become effective. Most notably, in Chapter 4 we reported that overall peer coaching in elementary schools had an effect that was not statistically different from zero. In the analysis in this chapter, we find some evidence that this overall zero effect is composed of a negative effect in 1999–2000 and a small positive effect in later years. Perhaps the second most important finding was that the overall negative effects of literacy block and block/core for EL students at the high school level may have disappeared by 2001–2002.

We also tested for, and found only scant support for, the notion that students who enroll in a given intervention more than one year receive disproportionately more or less benefit per year of enrollment than does a student who enrolls for one year only. This is particularly important because it reduces the chance that the reforms produced only transient Hawthorne effects.

Finally, we need to list two caveats to these results. First, sample size by year is smaller than in our overall samples, so that on occasion we find effects in given years to be insignificant even though overall across all years the results in earlier chapters showed effects to be significant. Second, it is tempting but inappropriate to project these trends into the future, thus inferring that the Blueprint may have become more effective with each year since 2001–2002, when our analysis ends. This hypothesis could well prove true, but it is just that, a hypothesis. It will take additional years of data to know for certain.

Those caveats aside, we believe that our results may indeed provide some initial evidence that San Diego has been "learning by doing." This seems all the more likely given the evidence presented by Stein, Hubbard, and Mehan (2004) of the difficulties that initially confronted San Diego administrators, instructional leaders, principals, and peer coaches in learning and then disseminating to classroom teachers the central ideas of the reading reforms.

7. Testing for Possible Side Effects of the Blueprint on Outcomes Apart from Reading

Introduction

As we stated in the introductory chapter, one initial public concern about the Blueprint was that its focus on reading would backfire by diverting students' attention from other subject areas. This potential seemed most likely in middle and high school, in which students have been directed to double- or triple-length English classes. However, those who read poorly may not learn much in their other subjects in part because their limited reading skills prevent them from reading their textbooks and related materials effectively. This hypothesis would suggest that time spent improving reading skills might actually increase gains in achievement in other subject areas than English.

A second potential side effect has to do with students becoming disenchanted with school because of the additional effort required in various Blueprint programs. Anecdotally, the San Diego media have reported complaints by several parents that their students were becoming "burnt out" by either literacy block and core, the extra-length English classes, or EDRP.

Lacking any firm evidence on either of these issues, we decided to test some of these propositions. Math and reading are the two core competencies tested at every grade level in which the state of California tests students. So we tested the "academic diversion" hypothesis by modeling gains in Stanford 9 math scores as a function of students' participation in the various Blueprint reading programs. It is obviously difficult to test fully the notion that Blueprint participation "burns out" students. We decided that the best approach was to model the percentage of days that students were absent in each year. Obviously this is a very imperfect proxy for students' attitudes, but especially in upper grades it likely reflects students' desire to be at school.

In both cases, we simultaneously controlled for all sorts of other factors that might have contributed to student outcomes. In particular, we continued to add student, school, home zip code, grade, and year indicator variables to our models. Probably the most important of these is the indicator variables for each student. These take into account unobservable but unvarying characteristics across students. Because of this, in practice we identify the effect of Blueprint elements by testing for a link between *changes* in a student's Blueprint participation and changes in the given outcome for that student.

Effect of the Blueprint Reading Elements on Gains in Math Achievement

We estimated models that mirror those in Chapter 4, except that the variable we were now trying to explain was gains in math scores rather than gains in reading scores. We used the corresponding vector of math teacher characteristics, peers' math test scores, and math class size in these models.[1]

Following the approach of Chapter 4, in Figures 7.1 through 7.3 we report the estimated effect of various Blueprint elements related to *reading* on gains in math achievement for elementary, middle, and high schools. The vertical axis in these figures, similar to those in Chapter 4, is the predicted percentage effect of a given Blueprint element on the average annual gain in math test scores. For instance, a bar in these graphs with a height of +10 percent suggests that the given Blueprint program is associated with a 10 percent increase in the annual average gain in math scores we observe for students districtwide.

Figure 7.1 suggests that for elementary school students, participation in various Blueprint reading programs, including schoolwide preventive strategies, is associated with quite big increases in the rate of gain in math achievement. The largest effect here is the introduction of a focus school

---

[1]This corresponds to model iv in Appendix B. Estimates using the sparser model i were also estimated, and the results were similar to what we report here.

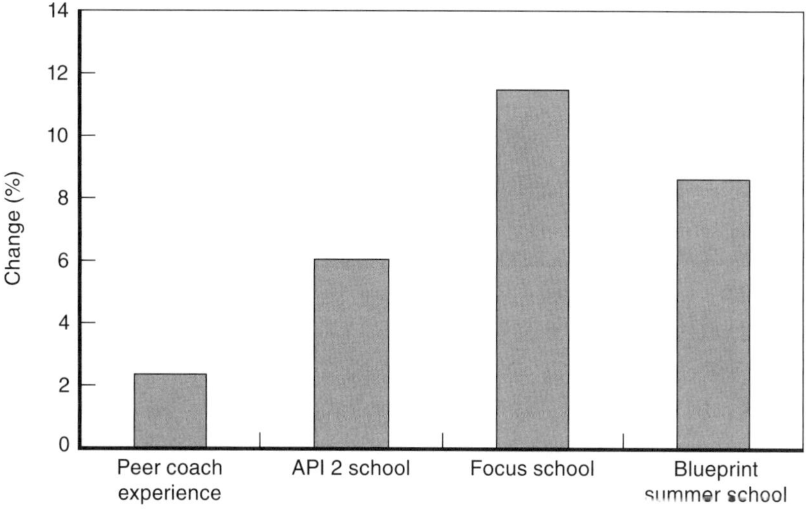

NOTES: For Figures 7.1 through 7.3, effects are simulated of a student participating in the given intervention or prevention strategy. Exceptions are nonbinary variables related to mean teaching experience of peer coaches, in which case we simulate the effect of a change from zero to the sample mean. For literacy core/block for EL students, we calculate percentage effects by dividing by mean math score gains for EL students.

Figure 7.1—Predicted Effect of Blueprint Elements on Annual Gains in Math Achievement Among Elementary School Students by Year

program at a student's school, which is associated with an 11.5 percent increase in the mean rate of gain in math scores. These findings are consistent with the idea that rather than taking student attention away from math, exposure to supplementary reading programs enhanced students' ability to absorb their math lessons. One variable that appears to matter for gains in math achievement, unlike in our earlier analysis of reading achievement, is peer coach experience. Figure 7.1 simulates the effect of increasing the average years of teaching experience of the school's peer coaches from zero to the mean actually observed, which for elementary schools is 12 years.

Figure 7.2, with results for middle schools, suggests a similar conclusion, with participation in a wide array of Blueprint interventions associated with gains in math learning for participants. Each of the positive predicted effects is quite big. Most notably, participation in

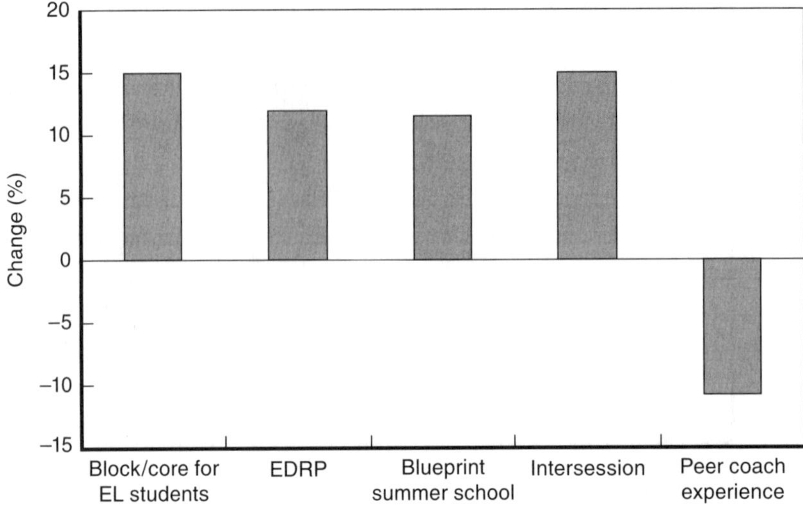

NOTE: See the notes to Figure 7.1.

Figure 7.2—Predicted Effect of Blueprint Elements on Annual Gains in Math Achievement Among Middle School Students by Year

block/core for EL students and participation in intersession are associated with 15 percent gains in math learning. One exception to the overall pattern is that schools at which peer coaches had more experience were associated with lower math gains. The predicted drop of about 10 percent is meaningful. However, this corresponds to a very large change in peer coach experience, from zero to the sample mean of 13.1 years.

Figure 7.3 shows results for high schools, which are quite different from those in the lower gradespans. Participation in literacy core for non-EL students is associated with a drop of about one-half in average gains in math achievement. EL students in literacy core/block are also predicted to learn less math, although this effect is far more muted. Finally, peer coach experience is modestly and positively related to math score gains. Overall, these high school results are the only evidence we could find that the Blueprint reading elements may have detracted from learning outside of reading, but they are quite dramatic results.

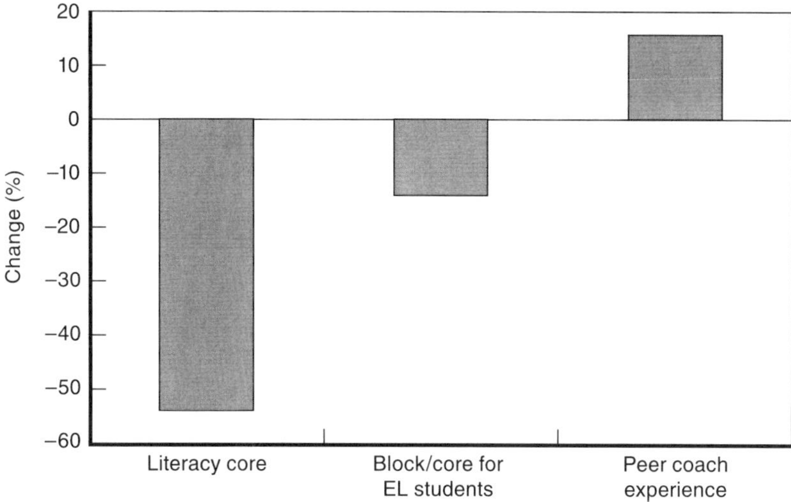

NOTE: See the notes to Figure 7.1.

Figure 7.3—Predicted Effect of Blueprint Elements on Annual Gains in Math Achievement Among High School Students by Year

Effect of the Blueprint Reading Elements on Student Absences

We tested the burn-out hypothesis by modeling the percentage of school days that a student was reported absent.

Figure 7.4 shows results for elementary schools. Each of the Blueprint elements that is statistically significant is shown in the figure, and each of these elements is predicted to have a negative effect on time absent. This is the opposite of what we would have seen if Blueprint programs were discouraging students from being at school. The effect of Blueprint retention (in grade 1) is particularly large: Students who are Blueprint-retained reduce their time absent by about one-quarter compared to the year before they are retained. This amounts to a reduction in the percentage of time absent of 1.2 percentage points, or about two days out of a 180-day school year.

We found far more mixed results for middle and high schools.

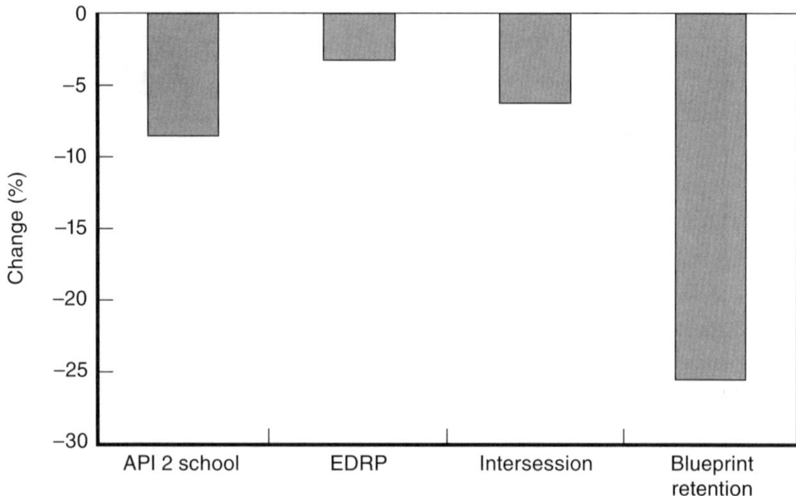

NOTES: For Figures 7.4 through 7.6, effects are simulated of a student participating in the given intervention or prevention strategy. Exceptions are nonbinary variables related to peer coaches as a percentage of enrollment and mean teaching experience of peer coaches. In both of these cases, we simulate the effect of a change from zero to the sample mean. For literacy core/block for EL students, we calculate percentage effects by dividing by mean math score gains for EL students.

Figure 7.4—Predicted Effect of Blueprint Elements on Time Absent in Elementary Schools

Figure 7.5 shows that various Blueprint elements are estimated to have had moderate, positive, or negative effects on time absent in middle schools. The last bar, in contrasts, suggests that Blueprint retention had a big effect, increasing time absent by 29.7 percent. This is virtually the opposite finding to the elementary school pattern. What does this imply in real terms? On average, middle school students were absent 5.0 percent of the time. Blueprint retention is predicted to boost these absences to 6.5 percent, or about 2.7 days out of a 180-day school year.

Figure 7.6 shows similarly mixed results at the high school level. Participation in literacy block is predicted to reduce student absences by a small amount. Peer coaches and apprentice peer coaches are predicted to have opposite effects on time absent. Overall, the simulated effect of going from zero peer coaches of either type to the mean percentages in

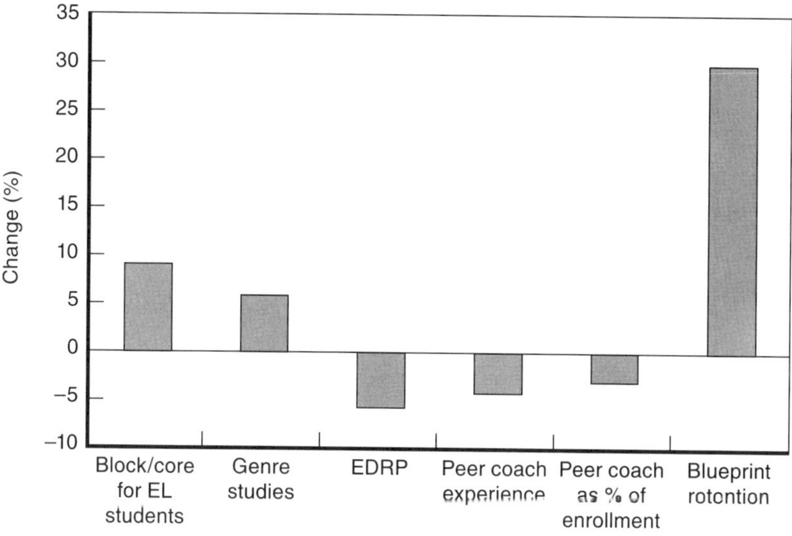

NOTE: See the notes to Figure 7.4.

Figure 7.5—Predicted Effect of Blueprint Elements on Time Absent in Middle Schools

high schools is predicted to alter time absent by –17.8 percent for regular peer coaches and +11.0 percent for apprentice peer poaches, for a net reduction in time absent of –6.8 percent. On the other hand, going from inexperienced peer coaches to those with the mean teacher experience observed in the district is predicted to increase time absent by 10.2 percent.

Conclusion

This chapter explores two possible side effects of the Blueprint reading reforms—"academic diversion" from math to reading and burn-out of students in terms of increased student absences.

Overall, this chapter finds little evidence that the Blueprint's reading programs have hurt math achievement. At the elementary and middle school levels, we in fact found the opposite to be true. These findings support the opposing hypothesis that reading ability is a "gateway" skill

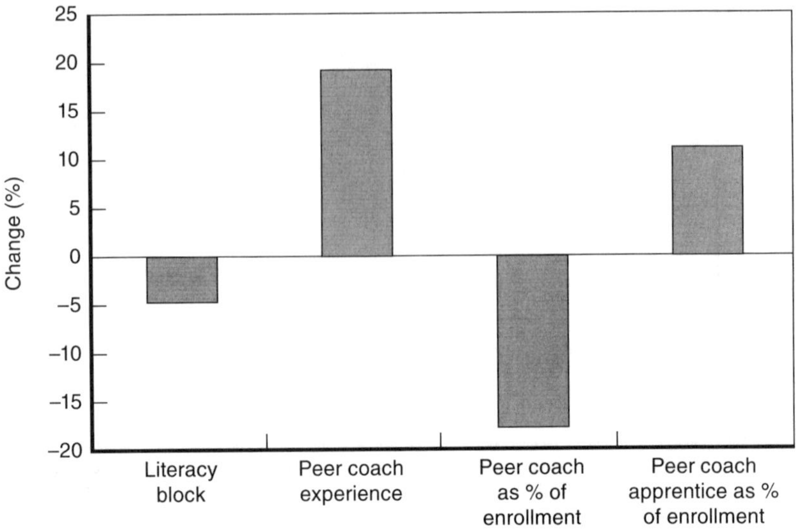

NOTE: See the notes to Figure 7.4.

Figure 7.6—Predicted Effect of Blueprint Elements on Time Absent in High Schools

that can foster student learning in other subjects. In contrast, high school results were mixed, but literacy core was associated with a drop of about one-half in gains in math. In a sense, this mimics the results for reading gains in earlier chapters suggesting the Blueprint reforms have had far more beneficial effects in lower grades than in upper grades.

Our test of the burn-out hypothesis suggested something quite different from student burn-out at the elementary school level, where student exposure to Blueprint reading reforms was uniformly predicted to reduce student absences. The estimated effect of Blueprint programs on time absent in middle and high school varied by Blueprint element, suggesting the lack of a consistent effect. However, even the most negative effect—a predicted 30 percent increase in time absent for middle schoolers who were Blueprint-retained, translates into an effect that is meaningful but not huge, specifically, a loss of about 2.7 days out of a 180-day school year.

Overall, then, we conclude that the Blueprint may have had beneficial side effects on learning in math in elementary and middle schools and on student absences in elementary schools. We expect that many readers will be surprised by these findings. Evidence of negative side effects crops up mostly at the high school level, but with the exception of a large estimated negative effect of literacy core on gains in math scores among high school students, these negative effects are quite modest. The negative finding related to literacy core at the high school level is consistent with results in earlier chapters on the effect of literacy core on reading gains at the high school level.

8. Conclusion and Tentative Implications for Policy

Introduction

A study of a major education reform should seek to answer several key questions, including "Which students participated?" "Did the reform work?" "How big were the effects?" and more policy-oriented questions such as, "In light of the evaluation, what should the district do now?" and "Are there lessons for other districts?" The preceding chapters have given detailed answers to the first three questions. Although we will briefly summarize these findings here, the main goal of this chapter is to focus on policy advice, such as it may be, both for SDUSD and for districts in California and elsewhere. These are particularly important tasks. In San Diego, the entire Blueprint is at an important crossroads. In winter 2005, the district's newly elected school board voted to buy out Superintendent Bersin's contract, and he departed on June 30, 2005, a year before his contract expired. Ironically, although Superintendent Bersin's early departure places the future of the reforms in greater doubt in San Diego, it also raises statewide and national attention on San Diego. The main reason is that on July 1, 2005, former Superintendent Bersin became California's new Secretary of Education, drawing observers across the state to speculate on what lessons he took from his San Diego experience and what statewide reforms he would subsequently recommend. So, what have we learned, and does it hold policy implications for SDUSD itself or for districts elsewhere more generally?

Patterns of Participation and Patterns of Effects on Reading Achievement

First, student participation in Blueprint interventions has been quite high, signaling the unusual scope of the Blueprint reforms. At the same time, the reforms have been rather focused in that the interventions have targeted students who lagged seriously behind in reading. Just under one-quarter of district students participated in at least one Blueprint intervention between summer 2000 and spring 2002. As expected, students who often fall behind in reading, such as EL students, Hispanic and black students, and students in schools serving relatively disadvantaged students, were much more likely to participate. In general, the district has used reading test scores to assign students to programs much as advertised. However, there is much flexibility built into the system.

Next, "Did the Blueprint work?" Our analysis suggests that student participation in many of the individual Blueprint elements has boosted student gains in reading achievement, sometimes in dramatic ways. The evidence that the Blueprint has worked is particularly strong at the elementary school level. Reforms at the focus and API 2 elementary schools as well as EDRP and Blueprint summer school were all associated with increased reading gains for individual students. We also find evidence that various Blueprint components at the middle school level have overall boosted student achievement in reading, although the gains are more modest than in elementary schools. Here, literacy block and core, EDRP, and Blueprint summer school are predicted to lead to gains in reading achievement. At the high school level, the overall effect appears to have been negative in the initial years of the reform—the only Blueprint element for which we found evidence of a positive effect was Blueprint summer school. Several other elements, especially literacy block for non-EL students and both block and core for EL students, were associated with *decreased* gains in reading achievement over the period we studied.

It is important to remember that each Blueprint element was in existence for one to three years during the period of our study and in most cases only two years. Had we been able to follow the reforms through spring 2004 rather than spring 2002, we might have seen different results. Notably, when we tested for differences in the effect of the Blueprint reforms by year, the most typical pattern was that the reforms worked better in later years.

Perhaps nowhere is this point more important than for high schools. Overall, during the 1999–2002 period, the Blueprint reforms appear to have had a negative effect at the high school level. But closer examination of the separate effects by year showed that the negative effect of literacy core and block had disappeared by 2001–2002, leaving two countervailing effects—a moderate negative influence of peer coach intensity and a large positive influence of Blueprint summer school. In other words, it would be premature to use our results to declare the Blueprint a failure at the high school level. Instead, our high school results imply some very large costs of introducing these reforms that were largely mitigated by 2001–2002.

As another example of the importance of the dynamics of the reform, the peer coaching program appears to have had no overall effect on student learning. However, we did find some preliminary evidence that peer coaching was beginning to have a positive effect in elementary schools by 2000–2001.

Beyond the question of "Did it work?" it is equally important to answer the question "Were the effects big?" We analyzed the size of the Blueprint effects in several ways. For students who participated in at least one Blueprint intervention between fall 2000 and spring 2002, the net effect was a gain in reading achievement equivalent to 22 percent of a standard deviation in elementary schools, an increase of 5 percent in middle schools, and a drop in reading achievement of 11 percent in high schools.[1] The size of these effects, at least for elementary school students, is quite dramatic. We also analyzed how Blueprint participants moved in the overall test-score distribution over this period. In elementary and middle schools, we detected a distinct movement out of the bottom two test-score deciles and into the higher deciles. For instance, we found evidence that the Blueprint had shifted roughly 10 percent and 5 percent of participants in elementary and middle schools, respectively, out of the bottom tenth and two-tenths of test-score performance into higher deciles. Again, the elementary school effect, at

---

[1]The standard deviation is a measure of variation. See Chapter 6 for more information.

least, is rather dramatic. In high schools Blueprint participation appeared to shift about 5 percent of students into lower deciles.

Side Effects?

We also investigated concerns voiced locally that the Blueprint's emphasis on reading would lead to student burn-out and diminish learning in other key subject areas. Our initial results partially cast doubt on these ideas. At the elementary and middle school levels, the Blueprint may have in fact improved math achievement, in spite of the Blueprint's initial emphasis on reading, and the Blueprint may have also boosted attendance in the elementary schools. The most negative finding we obtained was that in high school, literacy core was associated with substantial drops in math growth. Notably, the district has abandoned literacy core.

Implications for Policy in San Diego

Our analysis of the first two years of the Blueprint should be regarded as a preliminary and far from final judgment on the success of the Blueprint. Many studies of educational reform have shown that it takes several years for the full effects of reform to take root.[2] To be frank, we were quite prepared at the outset of this project to find no or only small effects of Blueprint reforms in the first two years. We were actually somewhat surprised to find effects as strong as we have in the initial two years.

What does seem clear is that the Blueprint has had far more positive effects in the lower grades, with elementary schools showing larger (positive) outcomes than middle schools, and high schools showing overall negative outcomes. An immediate policy question emerges: "Why did the results weaken in middle school and reverse in high school?" The weaker results in middle school than in elementary schools appears to be largely attributable to the whole-school elementary reforms

---

[2]For example, the considerable time and effort needed to make school reforms endure is a recurring theme in the collection of papers edited by Cuban and Usdan (2003b).

in the focus and API 2 elementary schools, which gave a large boost to elementary reading scores.

The larger puzzle is what went wrong, at least initially, in high schools. We offer four hypotheses. In middle and especially high school, students typically have different teachers for at least some subjects, whereas in elementary school, students typically spend most of their days with the homeroom teacher. It could be that the reading reforms work best when a teacher has the entire school day to observe the student's strengths and weaknesses in reading and writing.

A second possibility is that teachers in the earlier gradespans are more amenable to working with students on basic literacy skills than are high school English teachers, who by and large in San Diego have taken a rich medley of college English literature courses and who, presumably, are intent at least in part on teaching literature rather than teaching strictly reading skills that are the main focus of the state test.

A third factor derives from the notion that reforms take time, especially when they lack full historical precedent. Stein, Hubbard, and Mehan (2004) observe that the approach to reading that Chancellor Alvarado tried to adapt from his prior experience in District #2 in New York had been designed initially for K–4 and was later extended by District #2 staff to grades 5–8. The implication we draw is that reading reforms at the high school level in SDUSD built on less historical precedent than did the reforms in earlier grades, and thus they may take longer to fine-tune.

A final scenario, admittedly our most speculative, is that the double-length and triple-length pullout English classes created a negative stigma among struggling high school participants, who, like the typical teenager, hate nothing more than to be singled out in a negative way. One can see how the double-length and triple-length English courses would create stigma, particularly at the high school level, because the implication is that more periods spent in English per week must mean fewer periods in courses in other areas. This would potentially create an even bigger gap in the number of college preparatory courses taken in other subjects between those students in literacy block and core and other students. But it is not only the pressure to complete the so-called "a-g" college preparatory classes that would have heightened the stigma in high schools relative to middle schools. The general fear of stigmatization almost certainly rises as a student progresses through the teenage years. Anecdotal evidence suggests that one reason why nationally the percentage of students electing to receive federally subsidized school lunches plummets in the high school years is exactly the heightened and general fear of stigmatization among fifteen- to eighteen-year-olds compared to their younger counterparts. Indeed, it is interesting that the lone success at the high school level, Blueprint summer school, had a similar agenda to literacy block and core but was conducted in the relative quiet and anonymity of the summer months, rather than in the bright glare of the regular school day.

For San Diego itself, what are the main policy implications of our analysis? Perhaps the most useful way to infer tentative policy conclusions is to summarize and comment on how the district has altered the Blueprint since its formal inception in summer 2000.

The changes to the Blueprint reforms over the last few years have been legion. From the start, district officials have pored over test score results with a view to fine-tuning the Blueprint, and they clearly have sensed that overall test score trends in high schools have not responded in the same way as they have in lower grades. Partly in light of this recognition, as of 2004–2005 the district no longer offered literacy core in middle or high schools. In an interview with us in July 2004, SDUSD Superintendent Alan Bersin told us:

> I think our experience with the Blueprint, which your [PPIC] research bears out, is that the resource allocation strategy and the instructional strategies that we use . . . show a declining benefit as you move up the K–12 ladder. And certainly in the ninth grade through the tenth grade, we have not seen an appreciable increase in the graduation rate nor have we seen a significant growth in student achievement, notwithstanding the strategies that were in place, which involve the [literacy core] and so on. So about two years ago, we abandoned those strategies because the data didn't support that they were in any way having a sufficiently positive effect.

The district's board has also taken further measures, acting in 2005 to dismantle the peer coach program. And before that, beginning in 2003–2004, the district began to supplement or replace peer coaches with "content-level administrators" in literacy, math, and science. These content-level administrators are different from peer coaches in that they are less generalists and are more focused on subject matter knowledge than on teaching methods. Although it remains to be seen what effect these new administrators will have, it is certainly interesting to see that the district appears to be moving away from primary reliance on peer coaching.

It is also surely fair to say that between 2000 and today, California's school districts have felt continued financial pressure, especially in light of the state budget situation. The large cost of the Blueprint suggests that financial concerns considerably influenced the evolution of the reforms. Partly because of these cost concerns, the district severely curtailed EDRP in fall 2003, limiting central funding for these classes to students who are eligible under the federal NCLB act for supplemental services. To be eligible, a student must attend a school that is in the second year of Program Improvement status, and in addition the student must have low test scores. Preference is given to students eligible for meal assistance. EDRP has also been cut from 25 weeks to about 20 weeks to facilitate identification and placement of students deemed eligible under NCLB. Together, these two changes produced a considerable reduction in the EDRP.[3]

Blueprint summer school, on the other hand, has survived but now has limited spots available, again largely due to budgetary issues.

What do our results suggest about these cutbacks? Certainly, ending literacy core classes in high schools seems consistent with our finding that these triple-length classes were associated with lowered gains for individual high school students, especially if they were EL students. Even here, we need to emphasize that our findings from two years of experience do not necessarily imply the long-run effects of any Blueprint element, and indeed we found evidence that by the second year, literacy core had a zero, rather than a negative, effect on high school participants. Still, our results suggest that literacy core in high schools was initially among the least successful Blueprint elements. In contrast, we found that literacy core was associated with gains in reading achievement in

[3]In addition, a few school sites have apparently elected to keep EDRP and fund it through internal resources.

middle schools. Eliminating literacy core, especially in middle school, may have been premature.

Similarly, the recent cutbacks to EDRP seem unfortunate: This program was linked to gains in reading achievement in both elementary and middle schools, and the effects were meaningful. Moreover, the informal cost-benefit analysis we reported in Chapter 4 suggests that EDRP was probably significantly more cost-effective than another apparently winning reform, Blueprint summer school.

Our results do not provide strong advice on whether the district should have ended the peer coaching program. We did find some evidence that by 2000–2001, the peer coach program was starting to have a positive effect in elementary schools, but overall, we typically found no overall effect or slightly negative effects in elementary and higher gradespans. According to our analysis based in part on 2000–2001 financial data reported by the American Institutes for Research (2002), both EDRP and Blueprint summer school appear to have worked in a more cost-effective manner than peer coaching in that year.

To be fair, the argument we have made that reform requires time to take root perhaps is most relevant for the various professional development aspects of the Blueprint. In the case of peer coaches, they must absorb new teaching methods from their assigned instructional leaders and then must in turn teach these methods to individual teachers at their schools. It might have taken several years for this three-level hierarchy to transmit new teaching methods to the classroom most effectively.

Although the American Institutes for Research (2002) cost data do not separately report the costs of the preventive genre studies classes in the entry grade(s) to middle/junior high school, we note that unlike literacy core and literacy block in middle schools, we could detect no benefit of these double-length English classes for students near, at, or above grade level. Again, our findings may very tentatively suggest where to look for cost savings that could potentially restore some of the already curtailed Blueprint elements that do appear to work, such as EDRP in elementary and middle schools and literacy core in middle schools.

What about the troubling case of high schools? One possibility to improve outcomes at the high school level would be for the district to expand Blueprint summer schools on a trial basis in certain high schools. Such an expansion may be merited because Blueprint summer school was the sole Blueprint element that appears to have had a positive effect on high school students' achievement in the first two years of the program.[4] A second possibility, which we cannot guarantee would work, would be to experiment with a variant of EDRP in high school. This after-school reading program worked very effectively in lower grades, and it would be less controversial at the high school level than literacy block and core because it would not take time away from college preparatory classes in other subjects.

Policy Issues That Merit Further Study

Several key issues remain unresolved or only partially resolved by this work. Most obviously, further research will be needed to study how the Blueprint has fared in later years. We have studied the first two years of the official Blueprint; in 2004–2005, the Blueprint entered its fifth year of implementation. More subtly, in recent years the Blueprint expanded to encompass interventions aimed at boosting math achievement. This innovation represents a substantial addition to the reform's initial focus on reading achievement, and it merits study. Third, it will be interesting to study in more detail the cost-benefit aspects of the reforms. To be conclusive, such research will require additional years of data and more detailed budget information. Fourth, our initial study has found evidence that English Learners fared worse than other high school students in literacy block and core. With additional years of data, it should become possible to test for further variations in effect across various groups of students. Such variations could prove to be quite important for improving the selection of Blueprint interventions for specific students who lag behind.

---

[4]There is certainly room to expand: In 2000–2001, Blueprint summer school was available only to high school students in grade 9, with 14 percent enrolling; in 2001–2002, 23 percent of grade 9 and 11 percent of grade 10 students enrolled.

Take-Away Message for Local and National Leaders

This analysis of the first two years of the Blueprint reforms provides the first evidence available on the relative effect of the various elements of the Blueprint. For district policymakers, this evidence may provide some ideas for elements of the Blueprint worth preserving and for studying at the classroom level what aspects need overhaul. To the San Diego community, this report provides information that may quell some old debates and inspire some new debates. Overall, the various Blueprint elements have contributed tangibly to growth in reading achievement, and particularly in elementary schools the reforms appear to have produced impressive gains.

Clearly, the biggest disappointment in these initial results is that the large and positive results in elementary and middle schools have not transferred to the high school setting. Only Blueprint summer school appears to have worked as intended at the high school level. More research is clearly needed to determine why the reforms have worked less successfully in the higher grades.

For leaders in the rest of California and the rest of the nation, what do our results suggest? As Alan Bersin moves from San Diego to become California's new Secretary of Education, can he, and should he, draw upon his San Diego experience in promoting new statewide reforms? First, the results suggest that systemic education reform at all levels from the district offices down to the individual classroom and student can and does work. Second, they suggest that together the various components of the Blueprint might indeed provide one possible model for districts around the country, at least at the elementary and middle school levels. At the high school level, as is by now obvious, the same cannot be said.

Of course, several words of caution are in order to districts outside San Diego or outside California. To what extent are these reforms transferable? The most difficult question here is whether the most effective of the specific interventions, such as after-school reading programs and summer school, would have been so effective without the massive system of teacher professional development that was launched at the same time. We do not know the answer to this with any certainty, because the professional development was so widespread in the district that there is no obvious comparison group of schools that had the same student interventions but lacked professional development. Still, given the very limited effect of peer coaching that we observed in the district, we very tentatively infer that the reading programs such as EDRP and summer school would have succeeded at least partly without the full system of professional development created in the district.

A second note to districts elsewhere is that it is important to look at patterns of student participation in San Diego. Notions that the Blueprint interventions were mandatory are simply not true, as Chapter 3 demonstrates. Although school administrators could and did urge students identified as lagging behind to participate, parents could sign forms to keep their children out of the reforms. For instance, the *highest* participation rate we documented was for literacy block in 2001–2002, during which 70 percent of eligible students actually participated. This has important practical implications: The Blueprint interventions affected students whose reading scores made them eligible *and* whose families agreed to participate. There is no guarantee that similar results would have occurred in a system of truly mandatory interventions and, indeed, it is quite easy to imagine how a universal system of interventions could have produced effects that were either larger or smaller.

Overall, the Blueprint for Student Success has attracted widespread national attention and political and financial support from many individuals and groups outside San Diego. Initially, this attention was merited by the ambitious scope of the reforms alone. Now, looking back at the initial years of the Blueprint, we can say that this national attention was also merited by the fact that the Blueprint did appear to be boosting achievement and reducing achievement gaps between students, at least in elementary and middle schools. But at the high school level, the Blueprint did not yet appear to offer a mix of student services that is clearly effective.

Overall, the nation was right to put San Diego schools under a microscope. It will take careful assessment of several additional years of data on individual Blueprint elements to know for sure, but the promising early results in the lower grades suggest that the entire nation stands to learn important new insights about specific strategies for helping students to improve their reading achievement.

Appendix A

Data and Information on Blueprint Interventions

Betts, Zau, and Rice (2003) provide most of the details on our variables related to student background, class size, and teacher characteristics that we use to model gains in Stanford 9 reading test scores. Their data covered the school years 1997–1998 through 1999–2000. For the present study, we gathered similar data to cover the school years 1999–2000 through 2001–2002. One difference was that in 2001–2002 the district did a survey of all of its teachers, which led to updates to measures of teacher experience. In general these updates have increased the experience levels beyond the older measures of teacher experience that were based solely on administrative records. To this dataset, we added detailed measures of participation in various Blueprint interventions as well as schoolwide programs such as the hiring of peer coaches and the designation of certain elementary schools as focus or API 2 schools.

Participation in a Blueprint intervention depended primarily on test-score results. The interventions that used test scores as criteria for eligibility were literacy block, literacy core, grade retention, intersession, Blueprint summer session, and the Extended Day Reading Program. The following definitions describe what is considered "below grade level" and "significantly below grade level." On the SDRT, each exam is scored with a grade-level equivalent. The test-taker's current grade level is subtracted from this grade level equivalent. The difference is called the grade-level-equivalent difference. The value may be positive (above grade level) or negative (below grade level). The designation "below grade level" occurs when a student scores more than 1.1 below grade level on the SDRT. The designation "significantly below grade level" occurs when a student scores more than 3.1 below grade level on the SDRT. For example, if a student scored a grade-level equivalent of 6.0

and his grade level was 7.9, then his score would be –1.9 or 1.9 below grade level.

Literacy Block and Core Eligibility

Literacy block (double-length English class) and core (triple-length English class) eligibility is determined primarily by the prior years' test score results. Students in grades 4–11 (5–9 in 1999–2000) were required to take the SDRT. Additionally, students were allowed to take the ARI if their SDRT score was deemed inconclusive by their teacher. To determine eligibility fairly, both test scores were used and the highest grade-level-equivalent difference was kept to determine eligibility in literacy block and core classes. Literacy block classes are typically assigned to students who are below grade level but may be extended to those significantly below grade level in schools where literacy core classes are not offered. Literacy core classes are typically available to students who scored significantly below grade level in the sixth grade at middle schools, seventh grade at junior high schools (both beginning in 2001–2002), and ninth grade at high schools.

Eligibility Difference Between Middle and Junior High Schools

Current sixth grade students at middle schools who had nonmissing scores were eligible for genre studies or, if they scored below grade level or lower, were eligible for literacy block. Current seventh grade students at middle schools who had nonmissing scores were eligible for literacy block or literacy core, depending on their scores. Those below grade level would be assigned to literacy block, and those significantly below grade level would be assigned to literacy core. Current eighth grade students at middle schools who had nonmissing scores were eligible for literacy block if they were below grade level.

Assignment patterns were slightly different at junior high schools because the entry grade at these schools is grade 7 rather than grade 6. Current seventh grade students at junior high schools who had nonmissing scores were eligible for literacy block if they were below grade level. Genre studies were offered for these students if they were at or above grade level, but few students took the class.

Eligibility for EL Students

Current eighth grade (non-EL) students who had nonmissing scores at junior high schools were eligible for literacy block if they were below grade level. If they were significantly below grade level, they were eligible for literacy core. In high schools, current ninth grade students who had nonmissing scores were eligible for literacy core if they were significantly below grade level on the SDRT or ARI.

For EL students, the eligibility for literacy block and core is significantly different. Typically, a student's placement is determined by his test score as well as the number of years he has been enrolled at the district. Newcomers enroll in either literacy block or core, depending on what the teacher feels is best for the student. This makes it very difficult to determine whether a student was assigned to a class for a particular reason. Only twelfth grade EL students have the option of taking single-period English classes.

Summer School, Intersession, and EDRP Eligibility

Summer school eligibility is based on SDRT and DRA scores. A student who scored below or significantly below grade level on the appropriate exam is eligible for summer session. Students who fail a course are also eligible for summer session, although those students are not considered a part of the Blueprint summer school. All English Learners are eligible for Blueprint summer sessions, regardless of test scores.

Intersession is available at year-round schools that serve K–8 students. Students who are performing below or significantly below grade level are eligible for intersession, as well as all English Learners, regardless of their test score.

EDRP eligibility is similar to summer school. Any non-EL student in grades 1–8 who is scoring below or significantly below grade level is eligible for EDRP. EL students are automatically eligible and recommended to participate in EDRP.

Peer Coaches

Peer coaches are full-time teacher positions at each school designed to support literacy instruction. The peer coaches use a variety of strategies to help teachers in their classrooms, including co-teaching, demonstrations, observations, videotaping, and discussions of student work. An important role of the peer coach/staff developers is to provide support for beginning teachers. The coaches keep their knowledge and skills current by participating in coaching themselves, meeting weekly with their colleagues to discuss their work, and learning new strategies.

Peer coach information was obtained through teacher records. A Microsoft Access© query was created to search the California Basic Educational Data System (CBEDS) data for specific codes under the position title code. Those codes were 2070 and 2071 (2071 is the code for peer coach apprentice). The records were then merged with education records. Sometimes a school will get multiple records for peer coaches. This is because teachers were there at different times. Data cleaning methods were used to account for more than one record by keeping only teachers who served more than 90 days. The number of peer coaches as a percentage of enrollment was then calculated. Additionally, the average experience and education for all the peer coaches at a school were calculated. In the regression results presented in Appendix B, these percentages were further multiplied by 100 to allow for more convenient presentation of the coefficients.

Focus and API 2 Schools

Focus schools are elementary schools that scored in the lowest tenth on the state test. These schools received an extended school year, a second peer coach, and other funds and staff. Schools that were focus schools in both 2000–2001 and 2001–2002 were Baker, Balboa, Chavez, Emerson/Bandini, Jackson, Kimbrough, King, and Sherman. Schools that were focus schools in 2001–2002 only were Edison and Logan.

API 2 elementary schools scored in the second lowest tenth on the state test. They received a second peer coach and additional funds, but not an extended school year. The API 2 schools in 2000–2001 were Brooklyn, Chollas, Edison (which became a focus school in 2001–2002),

Encanto, Euclid, Horton, Kennedy, Logan (which became a focus school in 2001–2002), Marshall, North Park, and Perkins. The API 2 schools in 2001–2002 were Brooklyn, Burbank, Chollas, Encanto, Euclid, Garfield, Horton, Kennedy, Marshall, North Park, and Perkins. A list of both focus schools and API 2 schools was obtained through the department of Standards, Assessment, and Accountability at San Diego City schools.

Grade Retention

Blueprint grade retention differs from regular grade retention in that Blueprint grade retention is based on test scores whereas regular grade retention depends on overall annual progress as assessed by a student's teacher. Blueprint grade retention occurs only at grade levels 1 and 6/7, with the latter depending on whether the school was a middle or junior high school. Blueprint grade retention did not begin until the 2001–2002 school year as underperforming students were given a one-year grace period to catch up with their peers.

A list of students who were retained for Blueprint reasons at the first grade is compiled by the Office of Research and Reporting. Separate lists for students in the sixth and seventh grades are also kept. This office's data were merged with existing data using a student identification number. Variables were also created that denoted eligibility for Blueprint retention but do not indicate who was actually retained. During the first year of implementation, many students who were eligible were not actually retained because of miscommunication and misunderstanding regarding grade retention for Blueprint purposes. Hence, the number of students retained for Blueprint reasons is likely below the number who should have been retained. In addition, and by design, students can be exempted from Blueprint retention on a number of grounds. For instance, a student who had already been held back one or more grades was not Blueprint retained, and certain special education students were exempted as well.

Appendix B

Regression Methods and Results

As outlined in the text, we model gains in test scores, or $\Delta\text{Score}_{icgst}$ for student i in classroom c in grade g in school s in year t as a function of school, family, personal, and classroom characteristics. (Classroom characteristics include teacher characteristics and class size.) Our regression model is

$$\begin{aligned}\Delta\text{Score}_{icgst} = \alpha_s + \beta_{\text{Zipcode}_{it}} + \gamma_i + \text{Score}_{icgs,t-1}\omega + \mathbf{FAMILY}_{it}\text{E} + \\ \mathbf{PERSONAL}_{it}\Phi + \mathbf{CLASS}_{icgst}\Gamma + \mathbf{SCHOOL}_{ist}\Lambda + \\ \mathbf{BLUEP}_{it}\text{K} + \text{PEER}_{igs,t}\pi + \varepsilon_{it}\end{aligned}$$

where the first three variables on the right-hand side represent fixed effects for the student's school, home zip code, and also the student; $\text{Score}_{icgs,t-1}$ is the student's prior year score, added as a control for regression to the mean; the next four items in bold characters indicate vectors of time-varying family, personal, classroom, and school characteristics; $\mathbf{BLUEP}_{it}$ is a vector characterizing student i's participation in Blueprint interventions in year t, along with measures at the school level of Blueprint elements such as peer coach to enrollment ratios expressed as a percentage; $\text{PEER}_{igs,t}$ is the average test scores of a student's peers in his or her grade level at the current school, based on the prior spring's tests; corresponding Greek letters are vectors of coefficients, and ε_{it} is an error term.

Chapter 4 outlines the list of right-hand-side variables in the above equation, which we use to "explain" the variation in gains in test scores. One explanatory variable that deserves further explanation is the average test scores in a student's grade at the school. Suppose student i is in a school that has n students in the grade. Define

$$\overline{\text{Score}}_{g-1,t-1}$$

as the average score in grade g – 1 in period t – 1 for all students in the district, with $\sigma_{g-1,t-1}$ representing the standard deviation across all students in the district of the score in grade g – 1 in period t – 1. Then, in period t, we define

$$PEER_{igs,t} = \frac{\frac{\sum_{j \neq i} Score_{j,g-1,t-1}}{n-1} - \overline{Score}_{g-1,t-1}}{\sigma_{g-1,t-1}}$$

In other words, for student i in grade g in school s in year t, the average grade-level peer achievement variable is set to the average test score in the previous year for all of the other (n – 1) students in the grade at that school, minus the district average test score last year in the previous grade, and all of this divided by the standard deviation of test scores last year in the previous grade districtwide. So, a value of 1.0 for this variable means that the student's grade-level peers this year on average last year scored one standard deviation above the district mean. A value of –2.5 means that the student's grade-level peers last year scored 2.5 standard deviations below the district average. Betts, Zau, and Rice (2003) find strong evidence that these peer influences do matter for individual student learning.

The inclusion of the student fixed effects in the above model removes all unobserved but fixed influences on gains in test scores for the individual students. We believe that these models provide the most reliable estimates of the effect of classroom and other factors on student learning because they control for unobserved factors such as ability, motivation, and social norms in a neighborhood, to the extent that they are fixed over time.[1]

Our regression samples include students enrolled in grades 2 through 11 between the 1999–2000 and 2001–2002 school years. Our samples included 46,286 elementary school students, 34,037 middle school students, and 32,095 high school students, or 112,418 students overall. Together, the modeling of gains in scores and the use of student fixed

---

[1]See Appendix A of Betts, Zau, and Rice (2003) for a nontechnical explanation of the value of using such fixed-effect specifications.

effects means that a student must have three consecutive years of test scores in San Diego to contribute to the estimation of the Blueprint effects. Looking globally at district students, just under one-half fit that description. There are not more because the youngest students cannot possibly have taken the state test three times by the end of our sample, because testing begins in grade 2, and they may not have reached grade 4 by the end of our sample. But the main reason why about half of students do not have three consecutive test scores is student mobility in and out of the district. In a typical year in San Diego, just under 10 percent of students are new to the district, and a similar number have left. Simple calculations show that of all the students we would see in a district like this over a three-year period, about 60 percent are likely to have three test scores available, because of student mobility.

For this reason, our estimates of the effect of the Blueprint apply to students who remain in the district for three years. They may be less representative of students who have been in the district for less than three years. We did some checks on the demographics of attrition and found that blacks were less likely than other racial/ethnic groups to stay in the district three years, at a 42 percent probability compared to 46 percent for Hispanics, 49 percent for whites, and 57 percent probability for Asians, the most stable group. Similarly, 45 percent of EL students remained for three years compared to 49 percent of non-EL students. We cannot say for certain whether the influence of Blueprint participation for a given year would have been larger or smaller for our sample of students with three test scores. But it does seem likely that as a result in Chapter 5 we understate somewhat the net effect of the Blueprint because we undercount the number of affected students in our simulations of net effects over two years.

We need a reasonable number of students participating in a given Blueprint element to have a hope of detecting an effect as "statistically significant." We conclude from our earlier analysis of student participation that our dataset does not allow us to test convincingly for the effect of Blueprint grade retention because of a lack of student participation.

An important issue with these student fixed-effect models is how much variation there is in the Blueprint variables after we remove the mean differences among students by subtracting the student means. (This is an equivalent way to estimate fixed-effect models.) In almost all cases, we found that the standard deviation of our de-meaned Blueprint variables was about half, and sometimes as much as three-quarters, as big as the standard deviation in the raw data. In addition, the standard deviation after de-meaning was typically larger than the raw mean of the Blueprint element in question. This convinces us that there is sufficient variation in the data to support identification of the Blueprint elements, apart from Blueprint grade retention.

One main reason why we have so much variation in the data is that we include the 1999–2000 school year in our panel, which is the year before most Blueprint elements were introduced. However, as noted in Chapter 2, Table 2.1, one Blueprint element, peer coaching, was in fact widely implemented even in 1999–2000, with roughly two-thirds of students in schools that were served at least part year by a peer coach. But our overall measure of peer coach intensity, which is the number of peer coaches in the school divided by enrollment, shows a fairly large degree of variation before and after we subtract the means by student. The coefficient of variation (standard deviation divided by mean) in the raw data is 0.6, 0.5, and 0.6 in the elementary, middle, and high school data. After imposing the student fixed effect, we find a still respectable amount of variation, with residual coefficients of variation (defined as the standard deviation after de-meaning, divided by the mean of the raw data) being 0.4, 0.3, and 0.3, respectively.

We estimated six models for each gradespan (elementary, middle, and high schools). They proceed from very basic to models that successively add controls for class size (model ii), controls for teacher qualifications but not class size (model iii), controls for both class size and teacher qualifications (model iv), controls for class size and teacher qualifications and interactions between teacher experience and literacy block, core, and the various peer coach variables (model v), and controls for class size, teacher qualifications, and interactions between teacher experience and literacy block, core, and the various peer coach variables as well as interactions with Blueprint elements that occur outside the regular classroom (EDRP and Blueprint summer school). Tables B.1 through B.3 present these regression results.

The main results, presented in Chapter 4, are based on model iv, which includes controls for class size and teacher qualifications. Our reasoning for focusing on this model is that it is important to remove possible omitted variable bias by controlling for these measures that previous work by Betts, Zau, and Rice (2003) has shown to be related to student outcomes. If, for example, students in literacy block happened to be allocated the most highly qualified teachers, it is important to identify the effect of teacher qualifications separately from the direct effect of double-length English classes so as not to overstate the effect of the Blueprint. Obviously, the reverse correlation between teacher qualifications and literacy block classes would have led to us understating the effect of the Blueprint without including these controls. There is one sense in which model iv may "over-control" for non-Blueprint variables: By adding class size, we remove any benefit to students from the reduced size of grade 6/7 literacy block and grade 9 block and core classes. However, comparison of our various models suggests that controlling for class size in middle and high schools has almost no effect on our estimates of the effect of these Blueprint programs. Although we believe that model (iv) is the most conservative model of Blueprint effects, readers can judge for themselves the differences between this model and the more sparse models i through iii in the tables that follow. In general the differences are not large.

We estimated models v and vi to test whether the effect of Blueprint elements varied with the experience of the student's teacher. The results of these models are discussed in Chapter 4.

In Chapters 6 and 7 we present extensions to the basic model. The Chapter 6 models are versions of model iv that allow the effect of Blueprint elements to vary by year. In Chapter 7, we model student absences and math test score gains as a function of Blueprint participation. The sets of explanatory variables in these models are the same as in model iv with the important exception that for the math test score gains, we condition on characteristics of math classrooms rather than English classrooms, and in addition we use peer test scores for math, not reading. These models are not included in this appendix to save space but are summarized in the chapters themselves. Results are available upon request.

Table B.1

Regression Results for Elementary Schools

	Model i	Model ii	Model iii	Model iv	Model v	Model vi
Class size	No	Yes	No	Yes	Yes	Yes
Teacher qualifications	No	No	Yes	Yes	Yes	Yes
Interactions1: block, core, peer coach	No	No	No	No	Yes	Yes
Interactions2: EDRP, summer	No	No	No	No	No	Yes
Focus school	9.2838	9.2956	8.8184	8.8181	8.4197	8.2986
	(0.6890)**	(0.6906)**	(0.6944)**	(0.6962)**	(0.8162)**	(0.8184)**
API 2 elementary school	3.9351	3.9484	3.7652	3.7471	3.4959	3.3724
	(0.6025)**	(0.6046)**	(0.6061)**	(0.6080)**	(0.7375)**	(0.7404)**
Average years experience of peer coach	–0.0352	–0.0344	–0.0314	–0.0310	–0.0315	–0.0315
	(0.0163)*	(0.0163)*	(0.0163)	(0.0164)	(0.0164)	(0.0164)
Peer coach as % of enrollment	1.38	1.44	1.23	1.32	2.51	1.80
	(0.0197)	(0.0198)	(0.0198)	(0.0198)	(0.0221)	(0.0222)
Peer coach apprentice as % of enrollment	0.47	0.55	0.72	0.80	0.60	0.68
	(0.0143)	(0.0143)	(0.0144)	(0.0144)	(0.0145)	(0.0145)
EDRP participation	2.0197	2.0434	2.0147	2.0412	2.0308	2.6633
	(0.2848)**	(0.2857)**	(0.2847)**	(0.2856)**	(0.2858)**	(0.3828)**
Summer school participation	4.5938	4.6232	4.5009	4.5206	4.5379	4.7677
	(0.5504)**	(0.5509)**	(0.5506)**	(0.5512)**	(0.5515)**	(0.6333)**
Intersession participation	–0.8877	–0.8837	–0.8728	–0.8665	–0.9058	–0.8685
	(0.6737)	(0.6758)	(0.6739)	(0.6761)	(0.6765)	(0.6778)
Blueprint retained	0.0000	0.0000	0.0000	0.0000	0.0000	0.0000
	(0.0000)	(0.0000)	(0.0000)	(0.0000)	(0.0000)	(0.0000)

Table B.1 (continued)

	Model i	Model ii	Model iii	Model iv	Model v	Model vi
Interactions of Blueprint Variables with Teacher Characteristics						
Peer coach and 0–2 years experience					–1.4372	–0.0952
					(1.8871)	(1.9195)
Peer coach and 3–5 years experience					–0.1582	0.0382
					(0.7254)	(0.7357)
Peer coach and 6–9 years experience					–0.6342	–0.6058
					(0.4208)	(0.4287)
Focus school and 0–2 years experience					0.4468	0.8749
					(0.6102)	(0.6250)
Focus school and 3–5 years experience					0.2365	0.2645
					(0.2569)	(0.2619)
Focus school and 6–9 years experience					0.0651	0.0817
					(0.1553)	(0.1585)
API 2 school and 0–2 years experience					–0.0283	0.3921
					(0.6025)	(0.6203)
API 2 school and 3–5 years experience					–0.0268	0.0527
					(0.2217)	(0.2247)
API 2 school and 6–9 years experience					0.3668	0.3673
					(0.1566)*	(0.1594)*
EDRP and 0–2 years experience						–1.6397
						(0.4510)**
EDRP and 3–5 years experience						–0.1936
						(0.1583)

Table B.1 (continued)

	Model i	Model ii	Model iii	Model iv	Model v	Model vi
EDRP and 6–9 years experience						–0.0584
						(0.1023)
Summer session and 0–2 years experience interaction						–0.2181
						(0.5377)
Summer session and 3–5 years experience interaction						–0.2022
						(0.1862)
Summer session and 6–9 years experience interaction						0.0231
						(0.1210)
Number of observations	73,778	73,547	73,749	73,518	73,518	73,518
R–squared	0.73	0.73	0.73	0.73	0.73	0.73

NOTES: For a list of other regressors in the models, see Tables 4.1 and 4.2. Each column represents reading scores, using school and student fixed-effects models. Peer coaches and apprentice coaches as a percentage of enrollment are multiplied by 100. Standard errors are in parentheses.

*Significant at 5 percent.

**Significant at 1 percent.

Table B.2

Regression Results for Middle Schools

	Model i	Model ii	Model iii	Model iv	Model v	Model vi
Class size	No	Yes	No	Yes	Yes	Yes
Teacher qualifications	No	No	Yes	Yes	Yes	Yes
Interactions1: block, core, peer coach	No	No	No	No	Yes	Yes
Interactions2: EDRP, summer	No	No	No	No	No	Yes
Literacy block	1.7794	1.5230	1.3385	1.2475	1.3721	1.2134
	(0.3503)**	(0.3681)**	(0.3796)**	(0.4049)**	(0.5239)**	(0.5286)*
Literacy core	10.8149	10.5129	10.8654	10.4855	10.9528	10.3444
	(2.9076)**	(2.9104)**	(3.0919)**	(3.0949)**	(3.8973)**	(3.9074)**
Literacy block/core for EL students	0.9128	0.8262	0.4935	0.5552	0.5668	0.6196
	(0.4702)	(0.4717)	(0.5356)	(0.5386)	(0.5405)	(0.5415)
Genre studies	–0.0620	–0.1841	0.4853	–0.2061	0.5063	0.4691
	(0.5213)	(0.5240)	(0.5032)	(0.5399)	(0.6502)	(0.6513)
EDRP	1.2707	1.2901	1.1707	1.1823	1.1856	1.5699
	(0.3561)**	(0.3562)**	(0.3941)**	(0.3940)**	(0.3944)**	(0.4919)**
Summer session	1.5888	1.5894	1.5245	1.4937	1.5007	2.0217
	(0.3792)**	(0.3791)**	(0.4101)**	(0.4100)**	(0.4120)**	(0.5066)**
Intersession	0.8128	0.8373	0.5105	0.5610	0.5674	0.4835
	(0.5697)	(0.5698)	(0.6159)	(0.6159)	(0.6182)	(0.6199)
Average years experience of peer coach	–0.0144	–0.0132	–0.0129	–0.0146	–0.0135	–0.0131
	(0.0150)	(0.0150)	(0.0162)	(0.0162)	(0.0163)	(0.0163)
Peer coach as % of enrollment	1.48	2.16	1.96	3.05	3.31	3.08
	(0.0260)	(0.0262)	(0.0307)	(0.0311)	(0.0370)	(0.0370)

Table B.2 (continued)

	Model i	Model ii	Model iii	Model iv	Model v	Model vi
Peer coach apprentice as % of enrollment	–5.04	–5.44	–8.04	–8.43	–9.13	–9.05
	(0.0302)	(0.0302)	(0.0391)*	(0.0393)*	(0.0397)*	(0.0397)*
Blueprint retention	–6.0351	–6.0900	–3.0670	–3.1252	–2.9476	–2.7516
	(2.6309)*	(2.6308)*	(2.8736)	(2.8729)	(2.9439)	(2.9470)
Interactions of Blueprint Variables with Teacher Characteristics						
Genre studies and 0–2 years teacher experience					–1.2530	–1.2822
					(0.7217)	(0.7219)
Genre studies and 3–5 years teacher experience					–0.4174	–0.4088
					(0.3009)	(0.3010)
Genre studies and 6–9 years teacher experience					–0.1377	–0.1387
					(0.1355)	(0.1356)
Literacy block and 0–2 years teacher experience					0.0775	0.2947
					(0.4711)	(0.4798)
Literacy block and 3–5 years teacher experience					–0.0166	0.0452
					(0.1968)	(0.2035)
Literacy block and 6–9 years teacher experience					–0.1491	–0.1245
					(0.1216)	(0.1251)
Literacy core and 0–2 years teacher experience					3.5145	4.2534
					(4.4996)	(4.5117)
Literacy core and 3–5 years teacher experience					–0.9554	–0.7760
					(1.7554)	(1.7648)
Literacy core and 6–9 years teacher experience					–0.4897	–0.4224
					(0.8530)	(0.8576)

Table B.2 (continued)

	Model i	Model ii	Model iii	Model iv	Model v	Model vi
Peer coach and 0–2 years teacher experience					0.0531	0.0523
					(0.0626)	(0.0627)
Peer coach and 3–5 years teacher experience					–0.0714	–0.0694
					(0.0732)	(0.0736)
Peer coach and 6–9 years teacher experience					–0.0222	–0.0209
					(0.0762)	(0.0762)
EDRP and 0–2 years teacher experience						–0.0924
						(0.6524)
EDRP and 3–5 years teacher experience						–0.2108
						(0.2066)
EDRP and 6–9 years teacher experience						–0.1359
						(0.1085)
Summer school and 0–2 years teacher experience						–1.2463
						(0.5507)*
Summer school and 3–5 years teacher experience						–0.1814
						(0.2181)
Summer school and 6–9 years teacher experience						–0.0783
						(0.1258)
Number of observations	60,151	60,151	52,614	52,614	52,614	52,614
R–squared	0.70	0.70	0.70	0.70	0.70	0.70

NOTES: For a list of other regressors in the models, see Tables 4.1 and 4.2 and the discussion in Chapter 4 of the additional controls at the middle and high school levels for teachers' subject authorization and the number of English courses taken by each student. At the middle school and high school levels, teacher and classroom characteristics refer to the English classroom. Each column represents reading scores, using school and student fixed-effects models. Peer coaches and apprentice coaches as a percentage of enrollment are multiplied by 100. Standard errors are in parentheses.

*Significant at 5 percent.

**Significant at 1 percent.

Table B.3

Regression Results for High Schools

	Model i	Model ii	Model iii	Model iv	Model v	Model vi
Class size	No	Yes	No	Yes	Yes	Yes
Teacher Qualifications	No	No	Yes	Yes	Yes	Yes
Interactions1: block, core, peer coach	No	No	No	No	Yes	Yes
Interactions2: EDRP, summer	No	No	No	No	No	Yes
Literacy block	–1.1758	–1.2624	–1.1147	–1.2039	–1.3433	–1.4280
	(0.4025)**	(0.4043)**	(0.4074)**	(0.4094)**	(0.5085)**	(0.5101)**
Literacy core	–0.9455	–1.0349	–0.9231	–1.0154	–0.2536	–0.5678
	(1.1092)	(1.1098)	(1.1149)	(1.1156)	(1.6833)	(1.6932)
Literacy block/core for EL students	–4.2462	–4.2254	–4.1366	–4.1252	–4.0513	–4.0384
	(0.6386)**	(0.6386)**	(0.6440)**	(0.6440)**	(0.6451)**	(0.6452)**
Summer session	1.9009	1.8928	1.7627	1.7548	1.7657	2.6205
	(0.5748)**	(0.5747)**	(0.5764)**	(0.5764)**	(0.5775)**	(0.7684)**
Average years experience of peer coach	–0.0084	–0.0034	–0.0023	0.0011	0.0035	0.0034
	(0.0216)	(0.0217)	(0.0223)	(0.0224)	(0.0224)	(0.0224)
Peer coach as % of enrollment	–14.30	–15.43	–16.28	–16.73	–21.03	–20.79
	(0.0751)	(0.0753)*	(0.0779)*	(0.0779)*	(0.0844)*	(0.0844)*
Peer coach apprentice as % of enrollment	8.21	8.52	7.24	7.20	7.07	6.95
	(0.0474)	(0.0474)	(0.0489)	(0.0489)	(0.0491)	(0.0492)

Table B.3 (continued)

	Model i	Model ii	Model iii	Model iv	Model v	Model vi
Interactions of Blueprint Variables with Teacher Characteristics						
Literacy block and 0–2 years teacher experience					0.7359	0.8606
					(0.5288)	(0.5319)
Literacy block and 3–5 years teacher experience					–0.1715	–0.1522
					(0.2325)	(0.2345)
Literacy block and 6–9 years teacher experience					0.0197	0.0252
					(0.1193)	(0.1199)
Literacy core and 0–2 years teacher experience					–0.9834	–0.4718
					(1.4517)	(1.4712)
Literacy core and 3–5 years teacher experience					–0.6597	–0.5349
					(0.7943)	(0.8025)
Literacy core and 6–9 years teacher experience					0.3091	0.3472
					(0.4902)	(0.4974)
Peer coach and 0–2 years teacher experience					0.1493	0.1523
					(0.0813)	(0.0813)
Peer coach and 3–5 years teacher experience					0.0778	0.0798
					(0.1117)	(0.1118)
Peer coach and 6–9 years teacher experience					–0.0237	–0.0226
					(0.1074)	(0.1075)
Summer school and 0–2 years teacher experience						–1.8624
						(0.8506)*

Table B.3 (continued)

	Model i	Model ii	Model iii	Model iv	Model v	Model vi
Summer school and 3–5 years teacher experience						–0.3057
						(0.4491)
Summer school and 6–9 years teacher experience						–0.0508
						(0.2603)
Number of observations	50,677	50,677	50,677	50,677	50,677	50,677
R–squared	0.65	0.65	0.65	0.65	0.65	0.65

NOTES: For a list of other regressors in the models, see Tables 4.1 and 4.2 and the discussion in Chapter 4 of the additional controls at the middle and high school levels for teachers' subject authorization and the number of English courses taken by each student. At the middle school and high school levels, teacher and classroom characteristics refer to the English classroom. Each column represents reading scores, using school and student fixed-effects models. Peer coaches and apprentice coaches as a percentage of enrollment are multiplied by 100. Standard errors are in parentheses

*Significant at 5 percent.

**Significant at 1 percent.

References

American Institutes for Research, *Evaluation of the Blueprint for Student Success in a Standards-Based System*, Palo Alto, California, 2002.

Betts, Julian R., and Anne Danenberg, "An Assessment of Resources and Student Achievement," in Jon Sonstelie and Peter Richardson (eds.), *School Finance and California's Master Plan for Education*, Public Policy Institute of California, San Francisco, California, pp. 47–79, 2001.

Betts, Julian R., Kim S. Rueben, and Anne Danenberg, *Equal Resources, Equal Outcomes? The Distribution of School Resources and Student Achievement in California*, Public Policy Institute of California, San Francisco, California, 2000.

Betts, Julian R., Andrew C. Zau, and Lorien A. Rice, *Determinants of Student Achievement: New Evidence from San Diego*, Public Policy Institute of California, San Francisco, California, 2003.

Bohrnstedt, George W., and Brian M. Stecher (eds.), *Class Size Reduction in California: Early Evaluation Findings, 1996–1998,* CSR Research Consortium, *Year 1 Evaluation Report*, American Institutes for Research, Palo Alto, California, 1999.

Bohrnstedt, George W., and Brian M. Stecher (eds.), *Class Size Reduction in California: Findings from 1999–00 and 2000–01,* California Department of Education, Sacramento, California, 2002.

Clinton, William J., *1998 State of the Union Address*, January 27, 1998, downloaded from http://www.washingtonpost.com/wp-srv/politics/special/states/docs/sou98.htm.

Coleman, James S., *Equality of Educational Opportunity*, Government Printing Office, Washington, D.C., 1966.

CSR Research Consortium, *Class Size Reduction in California 1996–98: Early Findings Signal Promise and Concerns,* American Institutes for Research, Palo Alto, California, 1999.

CSR Research Consortium, *Class Size Reduction in California: The 1998–99 Evaluation Findings*, American Institutes for Research, Palo Alto, California, 2000.

Cuban, Larry, and Michael Usdan, "Fast and Top-Down: Systemic Reform and Student Achievement in San Diego City Schools," in Larry Cuban and Michael Usdan (eds.), *Powerful Reforms with Shallow Roots: Improving America's Urban Schools*, Teachers College Press, New York, 2003a, pp. 77–95.

Cuban, Larry, and Michael Usdan (eds.), *Powerful Reforms with Shallow Roots: Improving America's Urban Schools*, Teachers College Press, New York, 2003b.

Gootman, Elissa, "Fewer New York Schools Are Cited for Poor Performance," *New York Times*, January 5, 2005, p. A23.

Hanushek, Eric A., "School Resources and Student Performance," in Gary Burtless (ed.), *Does Money Matter? The Effect of School Resources on Student Achievement and Adult Success*, Brookings Institution, Washington, D.C., 1996, pp. 43–73.

Hess, Frederick M. (ed.), *Urban School Reform: Lessons from San Diego*, Harvard Education Press, Cambridge, Massachusetts, 2005.

Hightower, Amy M., "San Diego's Big Boom: Systemic Instructional Change in the Central Office and Schools," in Amy M. Hightower, Michael S. Knapp, Julie A. Marsh, and Milbrey W. McLaughlin (eds.), *School Districts and Instructional Renewal*, Teachers College Press, New York, 2002, pp. 76–93.

Jencks, Christopher, and Meredith Phillips (eds.), *The Black-White Test Score Gap*, Brookings Institution Press, Washington, D.C., 1998.

Jepsen, Christopher, and Steven Rivkin, *Class Size Reduction, Teacher Quality, and Academic Achievement in California Public Elementary Schools*, Public Policy Institute of California, San Francisco, California, 2002.

McGee, Maureen, "School Reforms Receive Grant Support," *San Diego Union Tribune,* November 6, 2001.

The National Commission on Excellence in Education, *A Nation At Risk: The Imperative for Educational Reform*, Washington, D.C., 1983.

Ochoa, Alberto, Op-ed in the *San Diego Union Tribune,* October 26, 2001a.

Ochoa, Alberto, letter to SDUSD Board Members on behalf of the San Diego County Latino Coalition of Education, October 9, 2001b.

Price, Hugh B., and Cecil H. Steppe, "The Achievement Gap Is Closing," *San Diego Union Tribune,* October 25, 2002, p. B7.

Quick, Heather E., Beatrice F. Birman, Lawrence P. Gallagher, Jean Wolman, Kassandra Chaney, and Hiroyuki Hikawa, *Evaluation of the Blueprint for Student Success in a Standards-Based System, Year 2 Interim Report*, American Institutes for Research, Palo Alto, California, 2003.

Sonstelie, Jon, Eric Brunner, and Kenneth Ardon, *For Better or For Worse? School Finance Reform in California*, Public Policy Institute of California, San Francisco, California, 2000.

Stein, Mary Kay, Lea Hubbard, and Hugh Mehan, "Reform Ideas That Travel Far Afield: The Two Cultures of Reform in New York City's District #2 and San Diego," *Journal of Educational Change*, Vol. 5, No. 2, June 2004, pp. 161–197.

About the Authors

JULIAN R. BETTS

Julian R. Betts is a senior fellow at the Public Policy Institute of California and a professor of economics at the University of California, San Diego. Much of his research has focused on the economic analysis of public schools. He has written extensively on the link between student outcomes and measures of school spending, including class size and teacher qualifications. He has also studied the role that standards and expectations play in student achievement. He is serving or has served on numerous U.S. Department of Education technical review and grant adjudication committees, two National Research Council committees, The National Working Commission on Choice in K–12 Education, and the national advisory boards of both the Center for Research on Education Outcomes at Stanford University and the National Charter School Research Center at the University of Washington. He holds a Ph.D. in economics from Queen's University and the M.Phil. in economics from Oxford University.

ANDREW C. ZAU

Andrew C. Zau is a senior statistician in the Department of Economics at the University of California, San Diego. Previously, he was a research associate at PPIC. His current research focuses on the determinants of student achievement in the San Diego Unified School District. Before joining PPIC, he was an SAS programmer and research assistant at the Naval Health Research Center in San Diego, where he investigated the health consequences of military service during Operations Desert Shield and Desert Storm. He holds a B.S. in bioengineering from the University of California, San Diego, and an M.P.H. in epidemiology from San Diego State University.

KEVIN KING

Kevin King is a doctoral candidate in the Department of Economics at the University of California, San Diego. Previously, he worked for the Board of Governors of the Federal Reserve as a research assistant. He holds a B.A. in economics from the University of Virginia and an M.A. and C. Phil. in economics from the University of California, San Diego.

Related PPIC Publications

Equal Resources, Equal Outcomes? The Distribution of School Resources and Student Achievement in California
Julian R. Betts, Kim S. Rueben, and Anne Danenberg

Determinants of Student Achievment: New Evidence from San Diego
Julian R. Betts, Andrew C. Zau, and Lorien A. Rice

Class Size Reduction, Teacher Quality, and Academic Achievement in California Public Elementary Schools
Christopher Jepsen and Steven Rivkin

School Finance and California's Master Plan for Education
Jon Sonstelie and Peter Richardson (editors)

PPIC publications may be ordered by phone or from our website
(800) 232-5343 [mainland U.S.]
(415) 291-4400 [outside mainland U.S.]
www.ppic.org